AN ARTS FOUNDATION COURSE

UNITS 1, 2 AND 3
INTRODUCTION TO HISTORY

Prepared by Arthur Marwick for the Course Team

The Open University

Cover: Drawing of Riddle's Close, Edinburgh, by James Drummond, 1854.
Photo courtesy of John Dewar Studios, Edinburgh.

The Open University
Walton Hall,
Milton Keynes
MK7 6AA

First published 1986. Reprinted 1988, 1989, 1990, 1991, 1993, 1994, 1995, 1996

Designed by the Graphic Design Group of the Open University.

Printed and Bound by Page Bros, Norwich

ISBN 0 335 11985 9

This text forms part of an Open University course. The complete list of units in the course appears on the back cover.

For general availability of supporting material referred to in this text, please write to Open University Educational Enterprises Limited, 12 Cofferidge Close, Stony Stratford, Milton Keynes, MK11 1BY, Great Britain.

Further information on Open University courses may be obtained from the Admissions Office, The Open University, PO Box 625, Walton Hall, Milton Keynes, MK11 1BY.

1.9

PREFACE

The Arts Foundation course is an interdisciplinary course in which, in Units 1–15, you will have a series of three-week introductions to the main disciplines (or 'subjects' as you probably called them at school) which make up the course: history, literature, music, art history and philosophy. As we go along we hope to show ways in which the disciplines overlap and interrelate. In Units 16–32 of the course we demonstrate the importance of interdisciplinary study (the fourth of our course aims) by bringing the five disciplines together in a study of 'Culture and Society in Britain 1850–1890'.

But we have to start off somewhere, and this course begins with my *Introduction to History*. I say 'my' because although this course has been planned as a unity by a course team (whose names you will find in the *Course Guide*), I want you to feel as you work through these first units, that I personally am talking to you, asking you questions, discussing your answers with you. What I talk about may be very different from anything you have learned previously about the study of history. What I shall be discussing with you will be what history is, how it comes to be written, methods used by historians, how *you* should read history, how *you* can distinguish good history from bad history, and how *you* should approach historical documents and, later, write history essays. In order to prepare you for the interdisciplinary study which forms the second part of the course, I shall draw most of my examples from Britain between 1850 and 1890. So that, apart from learning about the methods and purposes of historical study, you will also gain an introductory knowledge of Victorian Britain; however, as I am anxious to stress that the basic methods of the historian are the same whatever period he or she is studying, I shall also draw examples from well outside the Victorian period.

AIMS

The overall aims of these three units are:

1   To encourage you to appreciate that an understanding of the world in which we live depends upon an understanding of history.

2   To help you to appreciate that history is not simply an accumulation of facts but involves selection and interpretation; and to raise questions about the place of theory in historical study.

3   To awaken you to the richness and complexity of primary source material.

4   To introduce you to some of the fundamental problems involved in the handling of source material.

5   To make you aware of how history is written.

6   To provide the basic criteria upon which you can assess the relative merits of different history books.

7   To help you in the understanding and handling of periodization and of major problem words (for example, industrialization, class, culture).

8   To guide you towards intelligent historical composition of your own.

9   To introduce you to the interrelationships between history and the other arts disciplines.

OBJECTIVES

Introduction to History is divided into three units, each unit being equivalent to one week's work. Each unit is divided into individual sections. Each section sets out to achieve one basic objective, and should involve about one hour's work.

During them I shall be asking you questions, and I want you to make a genuine effort to write down answers in your notebook, keeping my own answers and discussions covered up. Detailed objectives will be given at the beginning of each unit.

PLAN OF THE THREE UNITS

Unit 1 The Nature and Purposes of History

This unit discusses the reasons for studying history, what history is about, how far historical writing can ever be totally unbiased, and the place of theory in historical study.

Unit 2 Basic Elements of History

First, this unit deals with primary sources, upon which all serious historical scholarship must be based, discussing their nature and range and the critical techniques that the historian brings to bear on them. Secondly, it discusses how historians interpret primary sources and the methods used to turn them into the history known to history students and general readers.

Unit 3 Problems of Writing History

This unit discusses in detail the problems of writing history both as encountered by the professional historian and by you as a student. It discusses some of the more important technical problems, in particular, periodization and historical semantics (or, in a more colourful phrase, 'historical hot potatoes') and suggests some of the ways in which you can distinguish between good and bad historical writing. There is a discussion of the relationship between history and the other arts disciplines.

SET READING

As you work your way through these first three units, you will need at all times to have beside you Geoffrey Best's *Mid-Victorian Britain 1851–75*, Charles Dickens's *Hard Times*, and *Culture and Society in Britain 1850–90: a source book of contemporary writings* edited by John Golby (Course Reader). Ideally, you should already have read the first two of these books, and during these first three weeks you will need also to read the chapters by Bédarida and Thompson in the Supplementary Material booklet.

You may very well find Best's tone hard to take at times. He's very much an academic's academic and at times gives the impression of addressing a rather limited audience of people who think and react like himself. It is perfectly proper to be critical of this, as it is proper to be critical of all books that you read. But do not let Best's little mannerisms stand between you and the important illumination of Victorian society which his book provides.

THE CHRONOLOGY

Nowhere in these units, nor anywhere else in the course (including the set books), is there a detailed point-by-point history of Victorian Britain. So have your chronology with you at all times: when reference is made to particular events, developments or persons, you will be able to place them by making reference to the chronology. Use the chronology also in conjunction with Unit 1, section 5, to gain an overall outline of the history of Victorian Britain.

BROADCASTING

The Arts Foundation course is a multi-media course in which the different elements are very closely integrated. Television, for example, is used to present those elements of the course which could not be presented effectively in any other way (visual evidence, paintings, buildings, music in performance, and so on).

Television programme 1 *The Necessity for History* relates directly to issues raised in Unit 1.

Television programme 2 *Witting and Unwitting Testimony* brings out the range and variety of sources in a way in which the printed unit simply cannot do, and goes into one of the fundamental points raised in Unit 2, the distinction between witting and unwitting testimony.

Television programme 3 *An Historian at Work* shows you an historian actually going about doing the things that are discussed verbally in the latter part of Unit 2 and in Unit 3.

Radio programme 1 *Interview with Lord Briggs on History.*

CASSETTE

You will need cassette 2, side 1, band 2 and the associated Cassette Notes to complete an exercise in Unit 2.

Unit 1

THE NATURE AND PURPOSES OF HISTORY

SET READING

As you work through Unit 1 you will need to refer to
Geoffrey Best *Mid-Victorian Britain 1851–75* (Set Book)
Chronology

BROADCASTING

Television programme 1 *The Necessity for History*

OBJECTIVES

Section 1 Definitions

You should understand that the word 'history' is used in various different ways: the 'history' we are concerned with is 'the historian's attempt to reconstruct and interpret the human past', not 'the past' itself. You should be able to distinguish between the different uses of the word 'history'.

Section 2 Justifications for the study of history

You should be able to list the various justifications which can be given for studying history and be able to discuss them in an informed way (you do not necessarily have to agree with them).

Section 3 The development of the modern discipline of history

You should understand the way in which history has emerged as a serious academic discipline in the last two hundred years or so.

Section 4 The basic concerns of the historian

You should have mastered the idea, as a starting point for your historical studies, that the three basic concerns of the historian are:

(a)   human beings in society;

(b)   change through time;

(c)   the particular and the unique.

You should also understand that history involves *explanation* and the study of the *interconnections* between events: *history* should be distinguished from *chronicle* — mere narration of events without explanation or interpretation. You should be able to distinguish history from other types of writing which occasionally bring in the past, such as sociology.

Section 5 Summary of the 'essential features' of Victorian society

You should understand that in coping with the vast mass of detail which confronts them historians necessarily summarize; and you should acquire a basic outline of certain 'essential features' of Victorian society, both as part of a continuing study of the basic concerns of the historian, and as a basis for later interdisciplinary study.

Section 6 The subjective element in history

You should be able to discuss intelligently how far all history is necessarily subjective and how far historians are in a position to limit the subjectivity of history.

Section 7 Theory in history: history as art, history as science

You should be able to take up a preliminary position on how far theoretical approaches are useful in history; you should be able to discuss how far history is a science and how far it is an art.

Section 8 An example of theory applied to Victorian Britain: class

Continuing from the previous objective, you should begin to develop a view on the relative value of Marxist and 'pragmatic' approaches to class.

Section 9 Historical research

You should understand what the scholar means by 'research'. You should also understand the crucial distinction between *primary* sources, the basic contemporary raw material of history, and *secondary* sources, interpretations written later by historians.

1 DEFINITIONS

Basically 'history' has two separate meanings. First of all it can be used to mean everything which actually happened in the human past (history is not concerned with the entire past, but only with that part of it which begins when human societies are formed), whether or not this has been recorded and interpreted. The second meaning of 'history' is the history that has actually been written down by historians. The first meaning is implied in the phrases 'what happened in history' or 'our most magnificent cathedrals are products of history'. Clearly cathedrals cannot be the products of something written down by historians. Much trouble would be saved if for this meaning we always used the words 'the past' or, more accurately, 'the human past'. But the fact is that words are often used to cover different meanings. Since there is nothing we can do about that, the thing is to be clear about which meaning is intended.

Here then is a fundamental distinction: 'history' as meaning 'the human past' and history as meaning 'historians' enquiry into that past and their attempt to produce an interpretation or reconstruction of it'.

Looking closely at the second meaning, we can make a further division of it. Throughout the centuries poets, singers, monks, even witch-doctors, have made some effort to present a version of the past, though usually without any very positive attempt to distinguish between fact and myth. It is only within the last two hundred years that history has developed as an academic discipline. Apart then from history as (1) 'the human past', the two other meanings are:

2 the uncritical attempt which has gone on throughout the centuries to present a version of the past;

3 the attempt to do this in a scholarly fashion, sticking to certain definite rules of establishing fact, interpreting evidence, dealing with source material, and so on.

From this second definition you will perhaps see how we come to use the word 'discipline'. When we speak of 'history' in this course, we mean history as the systematic, 'disciplined' study of the past. However, it is very difficult always to avoid using the word history in its other meanings, and I expect you will sometimes catch me, and probably my colleagues as well, using the word history when strictly speaking we mean the past. The important point, to repeat, is to be clear in your own mind which meaning is intended.

 Exercise

Listed below are various phrases involving different usages of the word 'history'. Identify which meaning is involved by entering:

A to indicate history as 'the past';

B to indicate 'the general attempt made by man throughout the centuries to describe, reconstruct, interpret the past which has been going on for centuries, and continues today';

C for history the academic discipline.
(If you are in doubt as between B and C, use B. Enter C only if you are absolutely certain that history as the academic discipline is clearly implied.)

1 'History should always be taught in the Faculty of Arts, not in the Faculty of Sciences.' ☐

2 'That television programme was very good as history.' ☐

3 'He preferred reading history to reading poetry.' ☐

4 'He preferred history to football.' ☐

5 'History is not the work of great men alone.' ☐

6   'Strictly speaking history is not a science.'   ☐

7   'Economic influences determine the course of history, not political ones.'   ☐

8   'We have had too much "drum-and-trumpet" history.'   ☐

9   'History is bunk.'   ☐

Answers and discussion

1 C	4 B	7 A
2 B	5 A	8 B
3 B	6 C	9 B

Remember the really important distinction is between *A* (history as the past) on the one side, and *B* and *C* (history as the historian's activity, whether scholarly or not) on the other. If at your first attempt you did not get the *B*s and *C*s properly sorted out this does not matter too much. But if you have *not* put an *A* for 5 and 7, or if you *have* put an *A* for any of the others, read the next five paragraphs, then go back and read section 1 again.

Unless 5 is meant to mean 'not all *historians* are great men' – and if the writer had meant this, he or she presumably would have said so – 'history' here must mean the entire past.

Seven refers to the past as it happened – not to the historian's reconstruction of the past – though if historians believed this statement to be true undoubtedly *they* would be influenced in the manner in which they write about the past.

Three might possibly be *C* rather than *B*, though since history is being compared to poetry, the activity of the poet, rather than to the discipline of literature, it seems reasonable to think that history in the broader sense is intended here. In the case of 4 it is more difficult to tell whether meaning *B* or *C* is intended, so that, in strict accordance with my instructions, *B* is the correct answer. With regard to 6, *C*, history the discipline, is implied. There would be little point in telling us that history in the broad sense, history without claim to exact scholarly method, is not a science.

The author of 8 (the Victorian historian, J. R. Green) meant the history of professional historians (*C*), but again the statement could apply to *B*, which, therefore, is the 'correct' answer (but you did well if you said *C*). Henry Ford (the famous author of 9) also probably meant the history of the professionals; but the professional historian (naturally) would probably argue that the remark is only applicable to unscholarly history. It would, of course, be nonsense to say 'The past is bunk'.

If you are still puzzled go back and once again read carefully through this section. Before proceeding be sure that you have grasped this business of the different definitions of history.

2 JUSTIFICATIONS FOR THE STUDY OF HISTORY

Why study history? This question is well worth thinking about, even if in the end you disagree with all the answers offered here.

Television programme 1, as its title indicates, suggests that there is not a lot of choice, that history is actually a *necessity*. The argument (which, of course, you may disagree with) is that no society could survive without a knowledge of its own past. This, certainly, would explain why right back to the earliest human societies, long before the development of history as a discipline, bards, witch-doctors, troubadours, folk-singers and monastic chroniclers preoccupied themselves with preserving and recounting stories of the past activities of a particular tribe, community or society. What they provided was the 'history' defined in the previous section as type *B*. It would appear that all communities need at least this type of 'history'. If history is necessary in this way, then it would seem sensible, in complex modern societies at any rate, for that history to be as accurate, as scholarly, and as disciplined as possible. It is in this way that I would argue for the essentiality of history as a discipline.

History (type *B* or type *C*) is to the community as memory (frequently not very accurate or disciplined) is to the individual. An individual suffering from loss of memory finds great difficulty in adjusting to other people, in finding his bearings, in taking intelligent decisions – he has lost his *sense of identity*. A society without history is in a similar condition. Thus the simplest answer to the question with which I began is: 'Try to imagine what it would be like living in a society where there was no knowledge of history at all.' History helps us to establish our identity, helps us to *orientate* ourselves, that is to say, to find our bearings. With a knowledge of history we find that instead of being totally adrift on an endless and featureless sea of time, we can establish where we are, and who we are.

The *necessity* for history is further brought out by the way in which in everyday life we are constantly stubbing our toes against the influences of the past or of interpretations of the past: consider the problems of Northern Ireland, or the attitudes of today's trade unionists, only comprehensible in the light of historical knowledge. Your environment – decaying towns, mean streets, magnificent cathedrals – is a product of the past.

Even if you ignore all this, prefer to look uninformedly at the buildings around you, never indulge in political conversations, nonetheless, much of your life is governed by what happened in the past, or sometimes by what people *thought* happened in the past. Television programme 1 indicates some of the relationships between British society today and what happened in Victorian Britain. It was made clear by Margaret Thatcher that she saw many of her policies as being based upon Victorian values; clearly it would be worth examining closely, and *historically*, these Victorian values.

Perhaps this justification for history as a necessity seems rather elaborate to you. You may have in mind other justifications for the study of history.

Exercise

Note down any reasons which you believe to be valid, or which you have heard other people put forward, for the study of history.

Specimen answer

Here is my list of most of the points which are usually made. Probably you have not got as many as this, and you may well have grouped some of the points in a rather different way.

1 History is enjoyable, just as enjoyable as the study of painting or music.

2 Among some people there is a simple 'wanting to know' about the past, a fascination with it – there is, one might say, a 'poetic' appeal about history.

3 History is an intellectual exercise, in the same way as any other intellectual pursuit, such as mathematics or philosophy. It thus provides a valuable 'training of the mind', and assists critical judgement and the systematic presentation of arguments.

4 History is a good form of 'humane' or 'liberal' education: it tells us about humanity in its various activities and environments and thus helps us to know and understand our fellow human beings.

5 History, being concerned with the totality of humanity's past experience, is central to all understanding of human beings and society.

6 History equips us to deal with the problems of the contemporary world.

7 History is part of humanity's continuing attempt to understand (and control) itself and its environment, physical and social; by contributing to our understanding and our control, it also contributes to our freedom as human beings.

8 Being fundamentally concerned with the study of evidence, history provides us with a specially valuable training in dealing with the deluge of conflicting evidence (in newspapers, on television, and so on) which assaults us all the time in everyday life.

9 To restate the justification I have already dealt with in full: history is a necessity.

10 History enables us to predict the future.

 Discussion

Obviously, some of these points overlap. Personally I would regard 5 as a restatement in more academic form (and therefore an extension and reinforcement) of my own basic point 9. But you might well regard 4, 5, 6 and 7 as saying rather the same thing in slightly different ways. Or, alternatively, 7 might be held to include at least two rather separate points within the one sentence. Equally, point 2 might be regarded as a special case of point 1; or one might (as I would) hold it to be part of point 9 (an individual expression of the argument that human beings *need* history); anyway, special commendation if you did make point 2 in some form or other, because it is essentially the reason given by Geoffrey Best on page 14 of *Mid-Victorian Britain 1851–75*.

Since we are dealing with the different justifications different people tend to give for the study of history, it is probably not worthwhile attempting a rigid categorization of what, in the end, is a personal matter. But I would like you to reflect carefully on this list for a moment or two.

To make my own position clear: I would regard point 9, together with its main corollaries (as I see them), points 5 and 7, as the fundamental justification for the study of history. I would regard point 8 as an important practical subsidiary justification.

 Exercise

Do any of the ten justifications seem rather dubious to you?

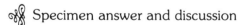 Specimen answer and discussion

I think we would have to rule number 10 out of court. So far the study of history certainly has not enabled us to predict the future, and most professional historians would argue that anyway this is in no sense the business of history. Point 6 might also be held to be rather strongly pitched. It is certainly part of my social necessity argument that history helps us to deal with the problems of the contemporary world, but it is scarcely true that history alone equips us to do this. History, one might say, would have to be taken in conjunction with a knowledge of the social sciences and, say, technology. Perhaps, too, you may feel that history (so far, anyway) is very far from enjoyable! Possibly you do not believe in the poetic appeal of history.

Anyway, as I say, these are fairly personal matters; but I do want you to reflect on them.

It is true that many famous historians, for example A. J. P. Taylor, argue that the only justification for the study of history is the first one, that it is enjoyable. Yet I want to put a question to you here on this point.

 Exercise

Even if historians themselves say that the basic justification for the study of history is purely its enjoyment, can you see how it could be argued that, despite what such historians say, nonetheless history does have a usefulness to society?

Specimen answer and discussion

The argument would run something like this. Even if a man says that he does something simply because it is enjoyable, it may still be that the activity (enjoyable to him) is *useful*, or indeed (as I would argue) necessary to society as a whole. The position is in fact rather like that of the artist who says he paints simply because he likes painting and that he is not interested in whether society needs his painting or not: even though *he* says this, it may well be that there is a basic human desire for art (or need for the illumination and insights great art may provide) which makes his paintings (*enjoyable* for him) *useful* for society. In other words, just because an individual historian justifies *his* study of history on the grounds that *he* enjoys it, that does not necessarily contradict the wider general justification that there is a social value in the study of history.

Exercise

Now just to see if you have grasped the various sorts of justifications that can be put forward for the study of history, I am going to list a number of statements about history which imply or correspond to one of the justifications for history already given, and I want you to put the appropriate number (1–10) in the box beside the statement.

(a) Britain paid a terrible price for the ignorance of the facts and trends of European history shown by her leaders before the Second World War.

(b) History is perhaps the greatest educational and cultural medium of our time.

(c) There exists in the human imagination an instinctive wish to break down the barriers of time and mortality and so to extend the limits of human consciousness beyond the span of a single life.

(d) History is the sextant and compass of states, which, tossed by wind and current, would be lost in confusion if they could not fix their position.

(e) The fundamental justification for historical study is its concern with the critical examination of sources.

Specimen answers

(a) 6   (b) 4   (c) 2   (d) 9 (or its corollaries, 5 and 7)   (e) 8

Discussion

These should be straightforward, but if you do not understand my answers, go back and read through this section again.

3 THE DEVELOPMENT OF THE MODERN DISCIPLINE OF HISTORY

What you should get out of this section is a clear idea of the main movements in historical study which have permanently affected the way in which history is studied and taught: positivism and Marxism are two outstanding examples of this kind of movement.

As we noted in section 1, historians of one sort or another have been at work from the beginnings of human society. And most people have heard vaguely of some of the more famous ones, such as Bede in the early Middle Ages, and Voltaire and Gibbon in the eighteenth century. In terms of definition *B* given in section 1 these men are great historians; nonetheless it is important that you should understand why history at the end of the eighteenth century cannot be regarded as a *discipline*.

Effectively there were three weaknesses in history as it existed at the end of the eighteenth century:

1   Although many scholars at various times had made brave efforts to base their work on genuine *primary sources* (the basic contemporary 'raw material', as distinct from histories written by other scholars – primary sources will be defined more precisely in Unit 2), there was no systematic use of sources and there were no accepted methodological principles. Among some of the great eighteenth-century historians there was a tendency to rely upon secondhand accounts rather than upon primary sources. To be fair, one of the problems affecting pre-nineteenth-century historians was that often important collections of documents – for example, documents belonging to kings or dukes or to the Papacy – were not open for inspection.

2   Eighteenth-century historians and most of their predecessors had very little real sense of the idea of change through time, of one age having particular and unique qualities of its own, different from those of another age. Both Gibbon and Voltaire had the habit of exercising their magnificent wit at the expense of earlier ages, criticizing the men of the middle ages for not coming up to the standards of civilization and behaviour expected of eighteenth-century high society. From the point of view of history as a serious discipline this is an unhistorical attitude, failing to see, in a well-worn, but useful cliché, that 'times change'; that the men of the middle ages should be studied on their own terms, not treated as an assortment of curiosities. Only with a developed sense of the idea of movement and change in history; only with a full recognition that each age is different from its predecessors, and its successors, and yet is at the same time worthy of attention and understanding in its own right: only then could there be a genuine discipline of history.

3   Though there was some teaching of history in the various universities, it was not organized in any very systematic way: the main emphasis was on Greek and Roman history or on legal history. The chairs of modern history established at Oxford and Cambridge in the early eighteenth century were exceptional, and their incumbents were essentially political favourites rather than genuine scholars.

It is widely agreed that the man who did more than any other to attack these weaknesses was the Berlin historian, Leopold von Ranke; though credit in the matter of pioneering the systematic study of primary sources should also be given to his Danish-born contemporary in Berlin, Barthold Niebuhr. Niebuhr's most important period of activity lay between 1810 and his death in 1831. Ranke turned his attention to historical scholarship in the 1820s and continued to write and teach for most of the rest of the nineteenth century.

Taking Ranke as the representative and leader of the Berlin school, let us glance at some of his more obvious achievements. First of all, he insisted that any piece of historical writing must be firmly based on the *primary sources*, and he made immense efforts to read as widely as he could in all the relevant archive collections before writing any of his many books (though he was fortunate in that it was just at this time that many of the archives, which had been closed to historians for so long, were now thrown open, at least to such favoured historians as the ultra-conservative Ranke). In the Preface to his first book, *Histories of the Latin and German Nations from 1494 to 1514*, Ranke (1824) made clear the fundamentals of his approach to history: 'The basis of the present work, the sources of its material, are memoirs, diaries, letters, diplomatic reports and original narratives of eye witnesses; other writings were used only if they were immediately derived from the above mentioned or seemed to equal them because of some original information.'

More than this, Ranke explained, the book would include the full scholarly apparatus (references, footnotes, bibliography, and so on, discussed in Unit 3, section 1): 'these sources will be identified on every page; a second volume, to be published concurrently, will present the method of investigation of the critical conclusions'.

Here we see, in brief but clear words, the very essence of the new scholarly emphasis, not only on primary sources but also on identifying these sources for the reader's benefit. And we also see Ranke's emphasis on 'method of investigation' and 'critical conclusions' – these words suggest, what Ranke certainly intended, that history was now presenting itself *as a science*.

It was in the same Preface that Ranke made another important statement which set the key for the modern discipline of history which is, in the first place, based on primary sources and, beyond that, concerned to understand the past on its own terms, from the inside as it were, rather than as 'an assortment of curiosities': 'to history has been assigned the office of judging the past, of instructing the present for the benefit of future ages. To such high offices this work does not aspire: it wants only to show how it actually was'.

This last phrase has often been quoted in mocking fashion, and undoubtedly Ranke was unduly optimistic in his estimate of how far study of the primary sources could yield an exact, objective, scientific account of 'what actually happened'. On the other hand this must be the *aim* of all scholarly history even if we admit that in the end subjective influences will never be completely overcome. It was Ranke's achievement, for all his defects, to set history firmly on this course.

Here, then, we see how Ranke attacked the first two of the weaknesses I listed above. Many other individuals assisted in this task. In fact the entire Romantic Movement (the artistic, literary and intellectual movement – personified by such novelists as Sir Walter Scott – which strongly influenced European thought in the early nineteenth century) fostered a great interest in the past involving both the attempt to see the past on its own terms, and the search for genuine sources dating from the past ('historicism' we shall term it when we come to the second part of the course).

Ranke played a particularly important part in countering the third weakness in historical study, being responsible for developing the systematic teaching of the new discipline of history at the University of Berlin, particularly through his famous seminars in which he instructed advanced students in the technique of using primary source materials. In general, other countries lagged behind Germany in instituting the systematic study and teaching of history. It is not really until the later part of the nineteenth century that history became established in the main universities (and therefore in the main schools) in the other Western countries. However, it can be said that by the end of the nineteenth century, history was firmly established as one of the most important subjects in all the leading universities. Almost everywhere 'history' meant *political history, diplomatic history* (foreign policy, the relations between different countries) or *constitutional history* (the study of organs of government, courts and parliaments).

Yet, while the particular approach to history pioneered by Ranke was making progress, a rather different approach to history was also developing in the middle part of the nineteenth century. With Ranke and his followers the emphasis was on the detailed accumulation of exact facts leading to a re-creation of the particular and unique events of the human past. Influenced by the great scientific advances of the nineteenth century, several leading intellectual figures endeavoured to create a kind of history that would be 'scientific' in the completely different sense of presenting general laws analogous to the laws of the natural sciences.

The first great pioneer of this approach was Auguste Comte (main period of activity, the 1830s), who is now widely regarded as the founder of modern sociology, but who left definite influences on historical study. Briefly Comte's idea was that the human past could be studied in just the same way as scientists study the physical phenomena of the natural world; he hoped to discover definite 'laws' of historical and social behaviour. For example, Comte formulated his famous 'law of the three states' which stated that the history of all societies and all branches of experience must pass through three stages, which he called the Theological, the Metaphysical and the Scientific. Comte's approach, which he called *positivism*, can be regarded as a valuable corrective to the studies of the Rankeans, which were so concerned with unique events and exact detail that at times they seem completely shapeless.

Even more important in developing an approach to history that postulated general laws and broad patterns is Karl Marx. (It may be helpful if I interject the personal point here that I am not a Marxist; simply, as a historian, I recognize the major contribution of Marxism to historical study.) Marx's writings are scattered over the period from the 1840s to the 1880s. Simplifying a little, however, it is possible to present a brief summary of the main lines of his thought: the *Marxist*, or *materialist conception* of history (sometimes also called the *Marxist interpretation* or the *materialist interpretation*, or simply Marxism – though when the word Marxism is used this may imply a political as well as an historical standpoint).

Marx first of all made a fundamental distinction between the basic economic structure of any society, determined by the conditions under which wealth is produced in that society, and the 'super-structure', by which he meant the laws, institutions, ideas, literature, art, and so on.

Secondly, he argued that history (in our very first sense of the word, history meaning the human past) has unfolded through a series of stages: *Asiatic, antique, feudal* and *modern bourgeois* – each of these stages being determined by the prevailing conditions under which wealth is produced (for example, in the feudal stage wealth is derived from ownership of land, in the bourgeois period it is derived from ownership of factories).

Thirdly, the motive force for this development from stage to stage is provided by the 'class struggle', classes themselves being determined by the relationship of particular groups to the specific conditions under which wealth is produced. For example, the bourgeoisie (or middle class) is the class which owns the means of production in modern capitalist industrial society. Previously it led the class struggle against the dominant group in the feudal stage, the aristocracy. Now (in the *modern bourgeois, or capitalist* period) it finds itself engaged in a struggle with the class below, the proletariat, or working class.

Fourthly, Marx argued that at the end of each stage a point is reached where new productive forces come into conflict with existing class relations, and then there begins, in Marx's own words, an 'epoch of social revolution'. There was 'social revolution' when feudal society gave way to capitalism; and there will be further 'social revolution' when capitalism begins to collapse.

Behind this view of the unfolding of history lies the notion of the 'dialectic', which Marx took over from the German philosopher Hegel – though Marx 'stood Hegel on his head' in applying the dialectic to material developments, not ideas. The basic notion is that each historical stage contains within it a contradiction which will lead on to the creation of the new stage – put crudely the notion of the dialectic means the confrontation between the two forces, the original historical stage, and the contradiction within it. Thus, according to the Marxian notion of the dialectic, or contradiction:

> ...the English Revolution of the seventeenth century occurred because the forces of production characteristic of capitalism had reached the point where their further development was held back by the feudal property relations sanctioned by the early Stuart monarchy; the outcome of the revolution was a remodelling of the relations of production which cleared the way for the Industrial Revolution a hundred years later. (Tosh, *The Pursuit of History*, pp.139–40)

From the point of view of the development of historical study, Marx is important for:

1   stressing the importance of economic history, of classes, and of work;

2   pointing a line towards interdisciplinary study, a history in which stress is laid on the interrelationship between art, ideas, politics and economics.

In the twentieth century, four of the most significant developments in historical study have been:

1   The development early in the century of an interest in economic history as a sort of specialist 'sub-history', analogous to the 'sub-histories' which the followers of Ranke developed in the nineteenth century; that is, constitutional history and diplomatic history.

2   The subsequent attempt to restore the unity of history (which seemed in danger of fragmenting into too many 'sub-histories') through the concept of 'total history'; a history stressing the interrelations between all aspects of man's past activities. The most important pioneers of this approach are two French historians whose work began just before the First World War, and who directly influenced historical study until after the Second World War: Lucien Febvre and Marc Bloch. In effect they founded what, named after the influential French historical journal, is known as the *Annales* school, which sees history as a social science and places great emphasis on such topics as the family, childhood, diet, social customs, social thought, and so on. The most famous *Annales* historian is Fernand Braudel, regarded by many as the most distinguished historian alive today.

3   The willingness to apply new methods and techniques to historical study, largely borrowed from the social sciences (including archaeology), but also from the natural sciences, resulting most recently in a 'new social history' employing both statistics and sociological theory.

4   In the last couple of decades or so, the development of a new, more sophisticated Marxism incorporating the inter-war writings of the Italian intellectual Gramsci, and the post-war methodologies of linguistics, structuralism, post-structuralism, semiology and hermeneutics. One famous figure you may have heard of is Foucault – though for myself I have to say that I regard him more as an imaginative, 'poetic' writer than as a disciplined historian.

 Exercise

Some of the statements below form reasonably adequate summaries of important aspects of the development of the modern discipline of history; others are false. Show that you can distinguish between the reasonable statements and the nonsensical ones by placing a tick in the box beside the accurate ones, and a cross against the inaccurate ones.

1   Marx was the true pioneer of the modern discipline of history.   ☐

2   Both Ranke and Comte claimed to bring science to the study of history, though in rather different ways.   ☐

3   Bloch and Febvre tried to prevent history from breaking up into a series of separate specializations.   ☐

4   Before Ranke there was no systematic university-level teaching of history.   ☐

5   Marxism, in the late twentieth century, has been completely replaced by new methods and approaches.   ☐

Answers and discussion

1   Inaccurate

Marx pioneered many things, but not this. If you got this wrong re-read the paragraphs about Ranke for his claim to be regarded as the pioneer of the modern discipline of history. (However, I guess a dedicated Marxist might disagree with me here.)

2   Accurate

Ranke meant 'science' in the sense of painstaking accumulation of evidence; Comte meant it in the sense of formulating general laws.

3   Accurate

If you got this wrong re-read what I have said about twentieth-century developments.

4   Accurate

If you disagreed re-read what I have said about the three weaknesses in history as it existed at the end of the eighteenth century.

5   Inaccurate

New approaches have developed quite independently of Marxism, but Marxism has also been adapted to developments such as structuralism.

4 THE BASIC CONCERNS OF THE HISTORIAN

These basic concerns are:

(a)   human beings in society;

(b)   change through time;

(c)   the particular and the unique.

4.1   HUMAN BEINGS IN SOCIETY

We have already defined history as 'historians' inquiry into the human past and their attempt to produce an interpretation or reconstruction of it'. A rather rigid distinction used to be made between 'pre-history' and 'history'. This distinction derived from the (correct) idea that since history (in the sense we shall be concerned with) is the historian's interpretation of the past, it can only begin to exist when the historian has reliable sources on which to base his or her interpretation. It was reinforced by the (dubious) idea that such sources must take the form of written records. In fact, as we shall see in the next unit, historians now call upon a much wider range of sources than mere written records, so that it is no longer worthwhile maintaining the rigid distinction between pre-history and history.

Most of our knowledge of the earliest human times is in fact the result of the work of archaeologists and anthropologists. But archaeologists have also made extremely valuable contributions to the study of quite modern times. So again it is silly to make a rigid distinction between, say, the periods of study appropriate to the archaeologist, and those appropriate to the historian.

Archaeologists have to possess deep professional skills to which the ordinary historian could not lay claim; yet, if we look at history in the very widest sense of the attempt to reconstruct the past, then archaeology (as many distinguished archaeologists have themselves said) is a form of historical study. It is not necessary to pursue this point further: all that has to be stressed is that beyond the simple fact that history is concerned with the study of the past, it is concerned with the study of human beings in society.

In a way the last two words of this statement are unnecessary: human beings *do* live in societies. However, it is best to keep these words in, since there has sometimes been an unfortunate tendency to write history as the exploits of individual figures, without reference to their social context. This is not to say that history should ignore the achievements of kings and generals, explorers and inventors. In one way or another such 'great men' have affected the development of hosts of lesser men and of whole societies and civilizations; they are therefore of great interest to the historian; but the historian must always have an eye on the wider implications: he should not study his 'great men' in, as it were, a vacuum.

4.2   CHANGE THROUGH TIME*

Man in society is also the concern of the various social sciences (anthropology, sociology, economics, political science and government, and so on). Sociologists and political scientists are naturally concerned with the problems of social and political *change*; yet, in the last analysis, the characteristic that marks history out from these other disciplines is a specific concern with the element of change through time. Putting it very roughly, the social scientist looks for the common factors, the regular patterns, discernible in man's activities in society; the historian looks at the way societies differ from each other at various points in time: how, through time, societies *change* and *develop*.

We shall return to these issues when we discuss the question of whether history should itself be regarded as a social science (section 7). Meanwhile what we are stressing is that history does in some sense *tell a story*: it must contain narrative, a sense of movement through time. Again, of course, we must not be too rigid about this: history requires explanation and analysis as well as narrative. A mere list of dates and events is a chronicle, not history: a writer of such a list is a chronicler or annalist, rather than in the fullest sense a historian. (Yet, while it is important that you should be able to distinguish mere chronicle from history, remember that because of this basic concern with change through time, the historian often has, as a fundamental and difficult task, to establish *exactly when* some events took place – we cannot *analyse* events until we know the exact order in which they took place.)

Sometimes the particular pieces of work historians set themselves will be exclusively concerned with analysis and explanation, and will not contain any explicit sense of change through time. But the historian will regard such work as contributing to the wider view of history in which there will be a sense of change through time. For example, one historian may devote his or her researches to a detailed study of what village life was like in England in the late thirteenth century: there will be analysis in depth, but little or no sense of movement through time. Another historian may similarly be occupied in a study of village life in the early fifteenth century. Before long a third historian will come along: putting these two studies together (no doubt along with other work of her own) to give a wider view, she will be able to bring out the *change* which has taken place between the late thirteenth century and the early fifteenth century.

That is to say, change over substantial periods, decades, generations, or perhaps hundreds of years.

4.3   THE PARTICULAR AND THE UNIQUE

The other point we have to make about history at this stage is that it must be concerned with what *actually did happen* to man in society in the past. In the examples just cited the historian will be concerned with what village life was like in the late thirteenth century and the early fifteenth century, rather than with making statements about village life in general. If he has studied enough examples of village life in different centuries, the historian may well decide to offer some broad statements about village life in general: but he must start off with particular examples. And even if the historian has a perfectly legitimate interest in what he believes to be recurrent patterns in human activities, he must always be sensitive to the uniqueness of past ages and events. There may or may not be patterns, but particular circumstances never recur in exactly the same way. It is a basic function of the historian to illuminate human experience by highlighting differences. Great historical writing will always be concerned with the meaningful interconnections and parallels between different events. But beware of historical writing that jumps over the uniqueness of past ages and past experiences in order to produce facile parallels and generalizations.

We shall return shortly to the question of general statements in history (section 7), but for the moment we should note this difference of emphasis between the historian and, say, the sociologist.

The historian is not, *in the first instance*, concerned to make general statements about human beings in society: he or she is concerned with the actual, particular, unique and different experiences which have befallen human beings in society in the past. Depending upon personal predilection he or she may *then* proceed to identify general patterns.

 Exercise

Consider very carefully Geoffrey Best's title, his table of contents, and also the remainder of his Preface, particularly the discussions on pages 15 and 16. From the table of contents we can see that Best is interested in 'the economic background', in local government, in public health, in people at work, in education, in religion; and from his Preface and various headings in the table of contents we can see that he is interested in class.

Here is a list of book titles that, in one way or another, touch on the topics dealt with by Best:

R. G. Lipsey *An Introduction to Positive Economics*

W. F. Cottrell *Energy and Society: The Relation Between Energy, Social Change and Economic Development*

J. G. Bulpitt *Party Politics in English Local Government*

W. J. Baumol *Welfare Economics and the Theory of the State*

Elliot Jaques *The Changing Culture of a Factory*

F. Machlup *The Production and Distribution of Knowledge*

Ninian Smart *The Religious Experience of Mankind*

Ralf Dahrendorf *Class and Class Conflict in Industrial Society*

Now my question (at last!) is: thinking in particular of Best's title, what difference seems to identify itself between his book and all of the books listed above?

 Specimen answer and discussion

Best's title is very specific: he is dealing with mid-Victorian Britain between two precise dates, 1851 and 1875. The other book titles are all rather general. They seem, to choose some examples, to be concerned with economics in general rather than with 'the economic background' in a particular country in a particular period of time, with the general nature of party politics in English local government rather than with specific examples of local government, with the theory of welfare economics rather than with public health (or poor relief) at a specific time and place, with the abstract 'production and distribution' of knowledge, rather than with specific educational institutions in a specific historical context, with class in industrial society in general, and so on.

Broadly speaking, while Best's title indicates clearly a work of history, the other titles suggest works in the various branches of the social sciences. History (though it may or may not be governed by some overall theory or theories – a question to be discussed later) is concerned with the specific, the particular, and the unique, rather than with the development of general theories or conceptual abstractions.

Of course, there is very fruitful overlap and interaction between history and many of the social sciences, particularly sociology and political science.

 Exercise

How does Best regard the interrelationship between history and sociology?

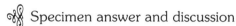 Specimen answer and discussion

Clearly Best regards history as being different from sociology, but sees it as open to the historian to *apply* sociological theory. While on the one hand regretting that he has not made more use of sociological theory, he also concludes that for his particular realms of interest sociological theory probably would not have helped him very much anyway. In particular, this is because he sees the social structure of mid-Victorian Britain as extremely complex and subtle and not amenable to division into precise social classes as (he believes) sociological theory would require.

5 SUMMARY OF THE 'ESSENTIAL FEATURES' OF VICTORIAN SOCIETY

Historians have to cope with an enormous mass of detail, some of it significant, some of it trivial. In presenting an interpretation within a relatively limited space of time, bringing out what is particular and unique, highlighting relationships between human beings and society, and clarifying elements of change, they necessarily have to summarize, to pick out what they take to be 'essential features'. As the study of Victorian Britain forms a major part of this course, I am now going to suggest six 'essential features' as headings under which we can conduct our study of Victorian Britain:

1   Basic features of the economy
2   Social conditions
3   Town and country
4   Industrialization and the social structure
5   Culture and belief
6   The major changes in Victorian society from the 1870s onwards

These headings will form a framework for our study of historical methods in relation to learning about Victorian society; from time to time, throughout the remainder of the units, I shall refer to them. In this section I shall add simply a few sentences and occasional questions on each heading. At the end of Unit 3 I shall repeat the six headings, providing a brief summing up and suggesting the way in which the headings relate to some of the documents in your Course Reader.

1   Basic features of the economy

 Exercise

Read Best's section on 'the Economic Background', pages 19–23. What does Best identify as the single most significant and indisputable feature of the mid-Victorian economy (that is, between 1850 and 1873)?

 Specimen answer

Best stresses Britain's economic ascendancy, its 'economic miracle', and the unprecedented degree and diffusion of wealth.

The question then arises of where this wealth came from, and since Best does not deal with this immediately, or in a very direct manner, I am going to simplify things for you here. Wealth came from three main sources:

(a)   Agriculture

Although you probably know something about the significance of the Industrial Revolution which began in the late eighteenth century and was already moving into a new phase by 1850, you should be sure to note that agriculture was still of great importance in the Britain of 1850, and continued to be important throughout the mid-Victorian period. You will get some measure of this significance from the tables Best prints on pages 99 and 100.

(b)   Commerce

Well before the Industrial Revolution Britain had developed as a nation of shopkeepers, wholesalers, auctioneers, bankers, insurance brokers, financiers, importers and exporters, and investors in foreign ventures. Best does not offer a precise heading for this range of activities, though the nearest one is 'Dealing' in the table on page 99. But even if something ought to be added from 'Transport' and 'Professional service', and all of what is contained in the heading 'Income from abroad' in the table on page 100, we can see that this is a relatively small heading, though continuously fourth in size, after 'Domestic service'. To get an impression of the importance of these activities as a source of wealth we would have to add the trade part of the 'Trade and transport' heading on page 100 to 'Income from abroad' to a proportion of the 'Professional' heading to the 'Rents of dwellings'. I stress commerce because it was the source of income for some of the most powerful figures in the land.

(c)   Industry

If we take this to include mining, building and transport, as well as manufacturing, we can see that it had by 1851 already established a dominant position both in respect of people employed and income generated.

2   Social conditions

As we have just noted, Best speaks of an 'unprecedented degree and diffusion of wealth', and undoubtedly one aspect of this period was that of both rising profits and rising wages. But as Best makes clear between pages 111 and 119, and elsewhere, Victorian society was also characterized by gross inequalities and deep pools of the utmost privation and misery. The two contrasting aspects of mid-Victorian society must always be kept firmly in mind. We come later to the detailed study of primary documents which will bring out, as only primary sources can, the direct reality of Victorian social conditions.

3   Town and country

From the statistics we have just noted demonstrating the dominance of industry, one might expect Victorian society already in 1850 to be highly urbanized, a society of towns. In fact, we must be cautious about jumping to any such conclusion. Best's table at the foot of page 24 makes it clear that it was only in 1851 that the urban population (54 per cent) outweighed the rural one. But then, if we go right to the foot of the page, we note that urban areas include places with populations of between 2,500 and 10,000 – scarcely more than villages, or certainly very small towns, by our standards. Thus while growing towns, and some very large ones, are important characteristics of Victorian society (and discussed very fully by Best, pages 23–84), it is important not to ignore the continuing importance of the rural areas (46 per cent of the population in 1851, 34.8 per cent in 1871, 29.8 per cent in 1881) and still more important to remember the significance of large villages and small towns still very closely interrelated with the countryside surrounding them.

4   Industrialization and the social structure

Despite the various qualifications I have been making about the importance of commerce, of agriculture, of small towns and of the countryside, it remains true that the single most important force of change in Victorian society was industrialization. By industrialization I mean the way in which, through exploitation of technology and the development of new industries and transport systems (the main ones are cotton and wool and textiles, iron and steel, coalmining, and railway building), people move from agriculture into factories, with all kinds of direct and indirect consequences, such as the growth of towns and changes in the social structure. By social structure I mean the way in which societies organize themselves into the very rich and powerful at the top, the very poor and powerless at the bottom, with various intermediate groups in between. Before the Industrial Revolution British society was organized into a long gradation of 'orders' or 'estates', moving down from the monarch through the various gradations of the peerage, to the country gentry, city merchants, gentlemen (such as clergymen, lawyers and doctors), prosperous tradesmen, and then a whole long catalogue of 'lower orders' including less prosperous tradesmen, small farmers or cottagers, artisans and craftsmen, labourers of many descriptions, domestic servants, and a vast army of unfortunates, paupers, vagrants and petty criminals. With industrialization we get a gradual reorganization of society into what are usually termed 'classes', and the emergence, in particular, of a 'middle class' and an industrial 'working class'. You will remember Best's recognition at the end of his Preface of his problems in dealing with class, so I shall leave elaboration of this important topic until later. For the moment I simply want to suggest the point that industrialization brings a gradual change from a society of orders or estates, to a society of classes.

5   Culture and belief

 Exercise

I wonder if you have any ideas about the Victorians, what sorts of things they believed in, and so on. I would like you to note down the sorts of ideas, beliefs and values you associate with the Victorians.

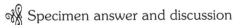 Specimen answer and discussion

I would expect you, perhaps with reference to certain speeches by Margaret Thatcher, to suggest some or all of the following: deep religious belief, belief in hard work and thrift, belief in self-help and personal independence, belief in the traditional virtues of the family, male superiority, and sexual abstinence (for women, at any rate). You might also have said things like strong national pride, patriotism, jingoism, imperialism, and perhaps also great optimism and belief in progress. Possibly you think of the Victorians as having clear and straightforward ideas about art and literature, unsullied by the complexities and obscurities of modernism. Or perhaps you think of the Victorians as being over-sentimental and debased in their artistic taste. Possibly you see the Victorians as having great respect for law and order, and for established political hierarchies. Or perhaps you think of the Victorian age as the dawning age of democracy.

Well, that's a mixture of some fairly positive statements, and also some potential contrasts and contradictions. Now I would like you to start with a very clear view of the way in which beliefs firmly held by a majority of Victorians were rather different from the sorts of beliefs which are widespread today. Undoubtedly, deep religious conviction pervaded society in a way in which it simply does not do today, with many accepting a completely literal interpretation of the Bible. Undoubtedly, many Victorians did have an optimism and confidence which it is difficult for us to feel, given the various batterings we have taken in the twentieth century, and particularly in recent years. But having stated that, and it is important not to retreat too far from that simple, yet basically truthful picture, I want to go on and stress that there were many ambiguities and paradoxes in Victorian culture and beliefs. Even at the very beginning of the period, there were those who doubted revealed religion. While economic success brought a general optimism and belief in progress, the violence and desperation of the dreadful slum areas of the large towns and cities brought also a sense of insecurity. Conditions of economic boom, as Best explains on page 19, led idealistic free traders to believe that 'international prosperity and concord' was at hand. Thus, while undoubtedly there was extreme patriotism and support for the kind of gunboat diplomacy associated with Lord Palmerston (Prime Minister, apart from an interval of a few months, from 1856 to 1866), there was also quite a strong vein of pacifism. Certainly the rich and the articulate did advocate thrift, hard work and self-help. Yet a basic utilitarianism (at its simplest, the highly functional view that whatever led to the greatest happiness of the greatest number was best, which came to mean that the straightforward efficiency reforms of Victorian Britain, private enterprise and better drains, were best) co-existed with an excessive sentimentality, a kind of debased romanticism. Finally, while the cause of representative government was advanced by the Reform Acts of 1867 and 1884, Victorian government continued to be highly autocratic and hierarchical.

6   The major changes in Victorian society from the 1870s onwards

Broadly I have so far been following Best in discussing mid-Victorian society, that is to say the period from roughly 1850 to roughly 1875. However, the interdisciplinary study which takes up the second part of this course extends from 1850 to 1890. The important question arises as to whether the basic characteristics I have been identifying can still be applied to the period after about 1875. ('Change through time', anyway, is a fundamental concern of historians.)

 Exercise

Best offers one answer to this question in his opening section on 'the Economic Background': what is this?

 Specimen answer

Best states (p.19) that 'the economic euphoria of the boom decades gave way to the relative ... gloom of the so-called Great Depression ... the conditions of international trade became less attractive for Britain'.

Later we shall consider in more detail the extent to which there was change in the basic features of the economy and, more importantly, how far there were changes in other aspects of Victorian society. For the moment, I want you simply to note that an important subject for discussion is that of how far late-Victorian society shared the same characteristics as mid-Victorian society, and how far there are clearly identifiable differences. Just to give you a few examples: it can be argued that the real dominance of urbanization and big cities comes in this period, together with an accelerated turning away from revealed religion, and the advocacy of new ideas such as increased government action in welfare matters.

6 THE SUBJECTIVE ELEMENT IN HISTORY

History is the historian's interpretation of the past. History, therefore, can never be completely objective ('objective' means 'unbiased' or 'strictly in accordance with the facts and uninfluenced by any personal feeling or prejudice'; 'subjective' means 'influenced by personal feelings'). Thus many people (especially those from a scientific background) find history an unsatisfactory subject. If history is merely personal interpretation or, worse still, pure propaganda, then it does not merit serious study. However, to admit the personal, subjective element in history is not to admit that history is no better than propaganda, or that it is simply a matter of opinion. Of course, some such criticisms may be made validly of *bad* history. But most of the remainder of these three units will be devoted to explaining the very rigorous principles and methodology upon which *good* history is based.

Opinion has fluctuated over the extent to which even good history must in some degree be subjective. The first great pioneers of history as a discipline, in the nineteenth and early twentieth centuries (see section 3), believed that they were creating a completely objective 'scientific' history, based on the strict study of sources. They believed that if you searched the sources in a thoroughly 'scientific' way, eventually the 'facts would speak for themselves' – without any need for subjective interpretation. In the inter-war years of the twentieth century there was a swing in a different direction: the facts, it was decided, would never 'speak for themselves' without prompting from the individual historian.

Today few historians would accept either of these positions: it is generally held that although the subjective element can never be eradicated, historians can, by the strict observance of certain principles, minimize the subjective element in their writing.

The subjective element which has received most attention is the one summed up in Professor E. H. Carr's famous phrase about history being a 'dialogue between present and past'. What is meant here is that each age tends to interpret the past in accordance with its own current prejudices and preoccupations. In the nineteenth century, when British political institutions (and above all the British parliament) were the admiration of the world, there was a very strong emphasis on political and constitutional history. Victorian historians of mediaeval England were obsessed with a desire to see in mediaeval institutions something analogous to a nineteenth-century parliament – though historians are now agreed that the 'parliaments' of mediaeval England were vastly different from those of the nineteenth century.

In their studies of the eighteenth century, and particularly of the reign of George III, Victorian historians and their successors interpreted the political intrigues of the time in terms of Gladstonian liberals versus Disraelian conservatives – something no historian has dared to continue to do since the publication of Sir Lewis Namier's celebrated studies of politics in the late eighteenth century.

In the twentieth century, as we become more and more preoccupied with economic and social matters, as we begin to give more weight to the mass of the people instead of just to kings and political leaders, the emphasis in historical writing has moved towards economic and social developments. Most recently there has been a flurry of work on women's history.

This 'present and past' dialogue can never be completely suppressed. Historians can never entirely escape from the influences of the age and environment in which they live. However, to a degree this is true also of the sociologist, the geographer, and even of the natural scientist. In the past, no doubt, historians have believed too readily that they were being scientific and objective, and completely ignored this 'hidden influence' of their own environment and preoccupations. But now that historians recognize this 'hidden influence' they are much better prepared to take action against it.

 Exercise

1   Recalling what has just been said about the inevitable subjective element in historical writing, comment in your notebook on these aims expressed by Lord Acton when in 1901 he was planning his *Cambridge Modern History* – a massive multi-volume collaborative enterprise between scholars of many lands (some of the names of these scholars are given at the end).

> Our scheme requires that nothing shall reveal the country, the religion, or the party to which the writers belong.
> It is essential not only on the ground that impartiality is the character of legitimate history, but because the work is carried on by men acting together for no other object than the increase of accurate knowledge.
> The disclosure of personal views would lead to such confusion that all unity of design would disappear...
> Contributors will understand that we are established, not under the Meridian of Greenwich, but in Long. 30°W.; that our Waterloo must be one that satisfies French and English, Germans and Dutch alike; that nobody can tell, without examining the list of authors, where the Bishop of Oxford laid down the pen, and whether Fairbairn or Gasquet, Liebermann or Harrison took it up. (Acton, 'Letter to contributors to the *Cambridge Modern History*', *Lectures on Modern History*, pp. 315–8)

2   What personal preferences come through strongly in the Preface to Best's *Mid-Victorian Britain 1851–75*?

3   Read, or re-read, Best's section on 'Lower-Class Incomes', pages 111–19: how would you characterize the tone in which this passage is written?

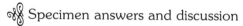 Specimen answers and discussion

1   These aims seem a little impractical since in calling for complete impartiality, for a history that will satisfy all religions and all nationalities, the writer seems to be ignoring the inevitable subjective element in history.

2   Clearly Best feels closer to students of literature than to students of the social sciences. Obviously he rejoices in writing 'social history of a rather old-fashioned sort', and clearly he is highly dubious about the value of sociological theory. It becomes clear that Best does not find the Marxist analysis of class acceptable.

These are predilections, inclinations and, to a degree, genuine reactions to the evidence as Best reads it. There is certainly no dangerous subjectivity here, but clearly in reading Best one would have to keep these preferences in mind.

3   I would characterize the tone of this as cautious, open and undogmatic. Best admits that the evidence on wage rates is incomplete and inconclusive, and thus he refuses to commit himself to more than the evidence warrants.

This, to me, is the entirely proper attitude for historians to take. In fact, where good historians are concerned the problem is not really so much that history is subjective, but that it must sometimes be slightly inconclusive.

 Exercise

Write a paragraph defending history against the accusation that it is a highly subjective subject and therefore unsatisfactory compared with, say, science or social science disciplines.

 Specimen answer

History does contain a subjective element. But this is true of other subjects, even science subjects, to a much greater degree than is sometimes believed: anything that brings in the human element, whether it be the setting up of a piece of scientific apparatus, or the carrying out of a social survey, must involve something of the human, personal element. What scientists and social scientists have to do is to try to cut down this subjective element to a minimum; and the same is true for history. In fact historians, being historians, have become increasingly aware of the subjective influences derived from the preoccupations and prejudices of the particular era in which they happen to live; historians are thus well equipped to be on their guard against these influences, even if they can never completely surmount them. What they cannot help is that the nature of their evidence sometimes prevents them from coming to firm conclusions. If historians admit openly that they are speculating, then they can be excused from the accusation of deliberate subjectivity. In the end history is the historians' *interpretation* of the past.

Discussion

Obviously your answer will not coincide exactly with mine, but if you have not understood the nature of the argument over subjectivity and history, and the defence of history which can be made, then you should read through this section once more.

7 THEORY IN HISTORY: HISTORY AS ART, HISTORY AS SCIENCE

Many scientists, some historians, and quite possibly you yourself, do not find the arguments advanced in section 6 persuasive. The only way, they would say, to avoid Best's shilly-shallying (his caution and openness, I called it), his literary flourishes and, to quote Best himself (page 14), his ' "unscientific" and "impressionistic" ' character is for historians to adopt some rigorous general theory. Then, as is usual in most science subjects, evidence which handled in the traditional way is imperfect and inconclusive, if interpreted in the light of a general theory will yield positive answers.

The general theory most acceptable to historians (though they remain a minority within the profession) is that derived from and refined from Marx and generations of Marxists commentators since. The desire to make history more systematic and more scientific is entirely laudable and is not always necessarily tied directly to strong left-wing political opinions. And there are indeed general theories, usually originating in the social sciences, which have been developed by non-Marxists, such as the theory of *modernization*. Marxist theory, at least in its more traditional forms (some branches of modern Marxist theory have become so complex and subject to qualifications that it is hard to distinguish them from non-Marxist approaches), maintains that it is an inevitable part of capitalist development for wages to worsen: thus Best's hesitations and perplexities would be resolved into a firm statement that they are entirely compatible with a long-term view of declining wages.

The modernization theory, on the other hand, has it that as industrialization with all its associated developments (according to the theory) of growing state powers, decline in religious belief, and development of a high-spending consumer society, advances it is inevitably accompanied by a rise in living standards. Thus Best's uncertainties would be resolved into a general long-term conclusion that wage rates were indeed rising. The upholders of general theory in history would argue that the methodologies which I describe in these three units are inadequate, that the historian's sources, however critically and professionally analysed, can never reveal more than the surface of events, and that there are deeper structures to human relationships which only some such theory as Marxism can expose fully.

In the end it will be for you to decide whether you prefer the pragmatic approach described in these units, to the theories of Marxism, or modernization, or whatever. It is important that you should know my personal position: though I disagree with Best on a number of points, including some aspects of his discussion of class, I do agree broadly with him that Marxist theories of class are not helpful in discussing the social structure of Victorian Britain (or of later periods). On the other hand, as I have noted in section 3, all historians since Marx have undoubtedly been influenced by his profound insights. Modernization can be treated as an interesting hypothesis (rather than a theory) against which evidence can sometimes be tested. I shall return to a more precise examination of Marxist and non-Marxist approaches to class in the next section.

One further point of possible confusion needs stating: to be sceptical about Marxist, or any other, general theory is not to deny the value (indeed the unavoidability) of concepts and hypotheses in historical study. In the second part of the course you will encounter a theory of cultural production which, within the specific context in which it is used, seems to me highly fruitful; theories borrowed from economics can be very useful in economic history as theories borrowed from sociology may be useful in social history; certainly historians cannot avoid conceptual generalizations such as *war, revolution, imperialism* and, of course, *class,* whatever the precise implications and assumptions they attach to each of these words.

When we ask whether history is or is not a science, we can have one of two issues in mind. Following Comte and Marx, we could be asking whether history has (or has not) a systematic body of theory (such as Marxism) or, following Ranke, we could simply be asking whether history is an organized and systematic body of knowledge with its own defined methodologies and disciplines. Many European intellectuals, using the latter definition, would regard history as a science.

However, there are certain obvious ways in which history, conceived in that way, does differ from most natural sciences, and perhaps also from the social sciences. I would list these as follows:

1   Historians cannot conduct controlled experiments or even the opinion surveys of social science.

2   Historians (though a minority would disagree with this), while they may need to make use of concepts and hypotheses, are not concerned with developing general laws or refining theory, but rather with the particular and the unique.

3   History, while it should equip us to cope more intelligently with the world in which we live, does not have the power of prediction.

4   There are times when historians simply cannot avoid making value judgements, even if no more than describing certain events as 'a massacre' or implying that certain practices contain elements of hypocrisy.

5   There are differences in materials studied: history is concerned with the human past, while the natural sciences are concerned with the phenomena of the physical universe and the social sciences, where concerned with the human past, use that past to draw out social theory applicable to the present.

6   In general, historians feel the need to communicate their interpretations in readable prose. This is why history is sometimes described as being 'an art' (as distinct from being an arts discipline), whether or not it is in addition conceived as being a science. It is true that we have pop science as well as pop sociology, but I think the point can be confirmed by a quick comparison between leading science and social science journals and any leading historical journal.

Exercise

Now read Best 'Religion and the Social Order' from page 190 to the end of the first paragraph on page 198, bearing the following questions in mind:

1   What notably 'unscientific' characteristics do you detect?

2   Is there anything that you would particularly identify as being 'scientific'?

 Specimen answers

1   (a)   The section opens with an elaborate metaphor. The likening of Victorian Christianity to a root running to seed, may well be illuminating, but it is literary rather than scientific.

(b)   Again, at the top of page 191, Best refuses to give, indeed almost seems to enjoy not giving, definite answers. Rather than appealing to either empirical evidence or to theory, he stresses the importance of 'judgement' or 'sense'.

(c)   In the next paragraph he makes some critical value judgements of certain Victorians.

(d)   The 'I imagine' at the foot of page 191 is scarcely scientific.

(e)   There is another value judgement, 'disunited and quarrelsome', at the top of page 192, and there is a subsequent implication of hypocrisy.

(f)   At that same point Best indicates that there might be a relevant social or political theory, but he is clearly quite determined not to make use of it, as again at the foot of the page he distances himself from any sociological line of enquiry.

(g)   Pages 193 and 194 make very agreeable reading (as indeed does the whole section, and most of the book) – this could be represented as history as art – but the information is perhaps somewhat miscellaneous and unsystematic.

(h)   The impression is perhaps confirmed by the three rather long quotations which follow from the foot of page 194 to the middle of page 196. These are interesting, but could be described as impressionistic – what hard evidence do they really give us, is it really of serious interest to know what Dickens thought (as distinct from what was widely and demonstrably true)?

2   The precise figures cited from page 196 onwards from the religious census do seem rather more 'scientific'.

 Exercise

We noted Best's specific disapproval of help from 'social and political theorists': what sort of theory does he seem to have in mind here?

 Specimen answer

The theory would be along the lines that religion is a social and cultural phenomenon, rather than a purely religious one, and that over a thousand years it had become a social institution so that people felt bound publicly to conform to its norms, not admitting to being wicked, giving money to charity as a matter of routine, and accepting professions and practice of faith at their face value.

8 AN EXAMPLE OF THEORY APPLIED TO VICTORIAN BRITAIN: CLASS

Broadly, the two main approaches to class boil down to this: the Marxist approach (which many historians, who in other respects would reject Marxist theory, accept as being the most persuasive view there is) sees class as a fundamental agent in the processes of social change; the pragmatic approach simply sees class as a means of describing or 'mapping' the way in which societies divide into society-wide social aggregates (a word less suggestive of complete homogeneity and unity than 'groups'), unequal in power and wealth, and distinctive in culture and life styles. To Marxists, the Victorian period was the one in which the industrial bourgeoisie, or middle class, took over from the aristocracy as the ruling class, leaving the way clear for a subsequent struggle between the proletariat, or working class, which would ultimately triumph, and the currently triumphant bourgeoisie. As things stood in the 1850s there were (to quote directly from Marx) three main classes:

> The owners merely of labour-power, owners of capital, and landowners, whose respective sources of income are wages, profits and ground-rent. In other words, wage-labourers, capitalists and landowners, constitute the three big classes of modern society based upon the capitalist mode of production. (*Capital*, Vol. III, pp. 862–3)

Marx recognized that there were other social groups or aggregates so that even in England 'the stratification of classes does not appear in its pure form', but to that he added that this was 'immaterial for our analysis'; and the *Communist Manifesto* had declared that 'the other classes decay and finally disappear in the face of modern industry', thus, of course, leaving the way clear for the capitalists and the wage-labourers.

In discussing class in nineteenth-century Britain, E. P. Thompson*, the most distinguished Marxist historian of that topic, has said that class is 'a relationship not a thing', that is to say the important point is the relationship of actual or potential conflict which exists between the classes, rather than any attempt to define precisely who belongs to what class.

The pragmatic approach, on the contrary, seeks to pin down exactly who does belong to what class, or social group, without believing that there must necessarily be a condition of actual or potential conflict between classes.

 Exercise

Read, or re-read, pages 15 and 16 of Best, and chapter 4 from the beginning (page 250) to the foot of page 292. In what ways does Best's analysis of class and social structure differ from the classical Marxist analysis?

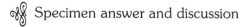 Specimen answer and discussion

In the Preface Best states quite clearly that he feels that the evidence suggests a much more confused picture of class structure than that offered by Marxist analysis; in particular he argues that there were far more gradations than the three main classes identified by Marx. He argues that the distinction between the Respectable and the Non-Respectable was more significant than the conflict between classes postulated by Marx.

In chapter 4 the main points made are:

1 Harmony rather than conflict was the dominant characteristic of British society in the period (p.254).

Not to be confused with F. M. L. Thompson whose work we shall meet in Units 2 and 3.

2   Best says it would be scarcely possible to imagine a less 'Marxian' worker than the self-improving and deferential artisan (p.258). (However, I feel bound to comment here that Marxist theory is perfectly capable of absorbing the notion of a prosperous upper crust of the working class – or 'aristocracy of labour' – which was happy to adopt the standards of the bourgeoisie. Best does at times seem a trifle naive in his understanding of Marxism.)

3   The vast majority of British people accepted contentedly the hierarchical structure of British society (p.260).

4   In particular the capitalist class which, in accordance with classical Marxist theory, ought to have been completing the overthrow of the aristocracy, was in fact, Best argues (pp.260–8), perfectly happy to go on being governed by the aristocracy.

5   The whole notion of the 'gentleman' on which Best lays stress (pp.268–78) really falls strictly outside any Marxist analysis. (But a Marxist could find in Best support for a Marxist analysis in which the idea of a gentleman is seen as an instrument of social subordination and therefore 'ideological' in the special Marxist sense of that word.)

6   Between pages 279 and 286 Best develops the argument already touched on in the Preface that the divide between the Respectable and the Non-Respectable was more significant than that between social classes.

7   Finally (pp.286–92) Best repeats the contention that mid-Victorian society was essentially characterized by harmony and cohesion, not by class conflict.

 Discussion

My complaint about Best would be that so anxious is he to stress the confusions inherent in the evidence, he leaves us without any very clear picture at all of the social structure of mid-Victorian Britain, beyond that it was 'more like that we commonly ascribe to the eighteenth century, of multiple gradations or ranks in a pyramidal order' (p.60).

Personally I think it is important for you to get firmly in your mind the way in which this eighteenth-century, pre-industrial structure was giving way to a new structure shaped by the forces of industrialization. I would emphasize the following points:

1   Some of the landed families as they existed at the beginning of the nineteenth century owed their origins and rise to power to commercial wealth, or to government or professional service, rather than to ownership of land; and many of them preserved close connections with large commercial families.

2   The commercial families of the City of London were already almost as powerful as the landed families.

3   However, there is no doubt, as Best stresses, that the aristocracy continued to be the dominant class in *mid*-Victorian Britain, and other classes deferred to it.

4   Successful industrialists certainly remained in an inferior position to these two groups throughout the mid-Victorian period.

5   By the late Victorian period one can definitely see commercial families and some of those professional families that could be characterized as 'gentlemen' beginning to merge into the landed class, to form a new upper class; the most successful industrialists were also joining in this process.

6   These developments left a very definite, though variegated, middle class of prospering, but less powerful and successful industrial and professional people who do not become part of the new upper class.

7   The Marxist notion of one class overthrowing, or replacing, another is wrong. What happens is that an existing dominant class, for example, the landed aristocracy with its associated commercial interests, *absorbs* the *most successful* members of the newly developing class – that is, those who were doing well out of industrialization in all of its aspects – and is then *modified* into something slightly

different, the upper class of the late nineteenth century which was still dominated by aristocratic and gentlemanly values, but which had very strong commercial and industrial elements in it.

This course does not insist on any one view of the class structure of Victorian Britain. It urges you to decide for yourself which view you find most persuasive. For the time being, the main point of this discussion is to illuminate for you the differences between a strongly theoretical approach and a strongly pragmatic approach.

9 HISTORICAL RESEARCH

'Research' is a word you will meet quite frequently these days. Often at the end of a television programme, in addition to the credits for cameraman and producer, you will see a little credit saying 'research by...'. What is meant here is that the material upon which the programme was based, as distinct from the organization and presentation of the programme, has been *discovered* by this 'researcher', who has consulted various books, sought information by personal interview, and so on.

This gives a slight clue to the meaning of research as used in the academic world. The clue is that research does involve *discovering* the basic material upon which a book, a thesis, an article, or even a television programme is based. There is no great harm in using the word 'research' in the loose way of the television programme-maker; and in fact you may, when, as a student, you are writing an essay, be tempted to say when you visit your local library that you are doing the 'research' for your essay.

But for the historian 'research' has a rather stricter meaning; and if you are to be able to distinguish between good history and bad history, you must have a very clear idea of what is involved in 'research', as the word is understood by historians.

Let me first of all try to say what is meant by research in this sense: research means *diligent and scholarly investigation in all the available primary and secondary sources, conducted not merely with the aim of 'making a book', but in order to extend human knowledge in a particular area.*

Now there is quite a lot here that needs explaining, first of all, the crucial distinction between primary and secondary sources. A *primary source* is a source that came into existence during the actual period of the past which the historian is studying; it is, if you like, the basic raw material out of which history (defined, let us remember once again, as 'the historian's interpretation of the human past') is made. A *secondary source* is the (or any) interpretation itself, written later by the historian looking back upon a period in the past. Roughly speaking one can say that the historian's function is to convert the raw material, the primary sources, into the finished historical product, the secondary source. This 'finished product' is still a source in that it will be used by other scholars, students and ordinary people with a general interest in history.

I said above that research must involve 'investigation in *all the available primary and secondary sources*'. The idea behind the second part of this statement is that no historian should embark on any subject without first having the common sense, and the courtesy, to try to master what his or her colleagues have written on that same subject. He or she may well find many interesting leads, and indeed pieces of concrete information, from these secondary works. But this work in secondary sources, essential though it is, is perhaps best regarded as merely a prelude to the real labours of research. For we certainly would not think very highly of an historian who stopped short after reading all the relevant books written by other historians. Usually we regard work as scholarly in proportion to its dependence upon study of the raw material, the primary sources (we saw in section 3, in fact, that one of the great achievements of Ranke in pioneering the modern discipline of history was this emphasis on primary sources).

In my definition I also said that investigation in the two types of sources (primary and secondary) should be 'diligent and scholarly'. It will be one of the main purposes of Unit 2 to explain the basic methodology which historians bring to bear on their *primary sources*, and upon which they rest their claim that their work is diligent and scholarly.

There is one further point included in my definition which you need not worry too much about at the moment, but to which I shall return when, in Unit 3, I discuss the value and the weakness of *pop history*. This is the point about research being concerned with expanding human knowledge, not just with 'making a book'. The difference here is one of aim and objective. The true researcher should have a genuine desire to increase human knowledge by exploring new territory. This aim is rather different from that of the author who thinks it would be rather nice to write a book, but has no particularly strong feelings on what he should write his book about, and in fact prefers to stick within the relatively easy territory of a topic which has already been explored quite fully by other historians. As we shall see later, one of the characteristics of pop history is that, very reasonably, it does not set out to increase human knowledge, but rather to communicate in a popular way knowledge that has been discovered by other historians. This knowledge discovered by other historians rests on what we can genuinely call *research*; if the author of a popular book talks about his research, he is using the word in the loose way mentioned above.

The important point is that research, truly understood, is directed towards exploring the unknown, towards *increasing* the sum of human knowledge, even if the increase may in itself seem rather small compared to the vast problems facing mankind.

It can happen that when a historian is concerned to increase knowledge on a rather large topic (such as, say, 'The Nature of Revolutions' or 'The Causes of Industrial Progress'), perhaps by illuminating new themes, or indicating new contrasts and comparisons, she will mainly depend on the secondary works of other authors; it may then still be reasonable to say that her work rests on *research*. For the moment, though, it is better that you should accept that *research*, as generally understood by historians, implies work carried out in *primary sources*.

This brings us back, then, to the point that we must be absolutely clear about the distinction between a *primary source* and a *secondary source*.

 Exercise

Here are titles, or descriptions, of various sources, primary and secondary, for a study of Victorian Britain. In the box provided place a *P* against the primary sources, and an *S* against the secondary sources.

1   Geoffrey Best, *Mid-Victorian Britain 1851–75* (first published 1971) ☐

2   *House of Commons Debates*, 1860–61 ☐

3   Hyppolyte Taine, *Notes on England* (1868) ☐

4   The (unpublished) diary of Francis Kilvert, Curate (1870) ☐

5   F. M. L. Thompson, 'The Decline of the Landed Interest', chapter 10 of *English Feudal Society in the Nineteenth Century* (first published 1963)

6   Sir John Seeley (Regius Professor of History at Cambridge University, 1880–95), *The Expansion of England* (published in 1883)

7   A. A. MacLaren, 'Presbyterianism and the Working Class in a Mid-19th Century City' in *Scottish Historical Review* (1967)

8   John May, 'Sanitary Measures in a Provincial Town' in *Transactions of the National Society for Promoting Social Science* (1857)

 Specimen answers and discussion

1 *S*	4 *P*	7 *S*
2 *P*	5 *S*	8 *P*
3 *P*	6 *P*	

If you have understood this section you should have got all of these right. The *P*s are 'raw material' originating in Victorian Britain itself; the *S*s are later interpretations. Seven may have given you difficulties, but coming from an academic journal published in 1967 it is quite definitely a *secondary* source. Source 6 is perhaps the most difficult of all, because as a contemporary history (discussed in Unit 2) and a secondary source in its own day, it contains large elements of secondary interpretation, but since it originates in the period studied it is basically a primary source, giving us direct insights into attitudes towards the empire. If you have any doubts, read through this section again.

 Exercise

Geoffrey Best says of *Mid-Victorian Britain 1851–75* that it 'is not much of a work of "research", as conventionally understood' (p.16). What does he mean by this?

Specimen answer

He means that his book is largely drawn from the secondary works of others, rather than being mainly based on primary sources as we would expect of a true work of research.

REFERENCES

Acton, Lord (1952) 'Letter to contributors to the *Cambridge Modern History'*, *Lectures on Modern History* (Macmillan).

Best, G. (1979) *Mid-Victorian Britain 1851–75*, Fontana.

Marx, K. (1938 edition) *Capital*, Allen.

Tosh, J. (1984) *The Pursuit of History*, Longman.

Von Ranke, L. (1824) *Histories of the Latin and German Nations from 1494 to 1514*.

Unit 2

BASIC ELEMENTS OF HISTORY

SET READING

As you work through Unit 2 you will need to refer to
John Golby (ed.) (1986) *Culture and Society in Britain 1850–1890* (Course Reader)
Geoffrey Best (1979) *Mid-Victorian Britain 1851–75* (Set Book)
Charles Dickens (1989 edition) *Hard Times* (Set Book)
Supplementary Material booklet
Cassette Notes

BROADCASTING

Television programme 2 *Witting and Unwitting Testimony*
Television programme 3 *An Historian at Work*
Radio programme 1 *Interview with Lord Briggs on History*

CASSETTE

Cassette 2, side 1, band 2

OBJECTIVES

Section 1 The variety of primary sources

You should appreciate the variety and range of primary sources, which include archaeological remains, aerial photographs, archive film, and so on, as well as the more obvious written sources.

Section 2 Witting and unwitting testimony

You should understand the fundamental distinction between the *witting testimony* of a primary source – the information which the original writer or creator of the source deliberately intended to convey to his own contemporaries – and the *unwitting testimony* – the information which the historian extracts from the source (about attitudes, assumptions, values, and so on) which was in no way intended by the original writer.

Section 3 Criticism and evaluation of primary sources

You should be aware of the methods and techniques that the historian brings to bear on his primary sources.

Section 4 Literature and art as primary sources

You should appreciate the special value and the special dangers of this type of source.

Section 5 The imperfect and fragmentary nature of historical sources

You should understand that the sources upon which historians depend are extremely fragmentary and imperfect, and often very difficult to draw any clear, positive conclusions from at all.

Section 6 Communication

You should appreciate that apart from *research* the historian must be concerned with communicating his findings.

Section 7 The basic elements of form and structure in historical writing

You should yourself, when writing any sort of history, know how to communicate in the clearest and best way.

Section 8 Selection in historical writing

You should know what to leave out when you are writing any kind of history.

Section 9 Narrative, analysis and description

To help you in your own writing, and to help you in reading works by other historians, you should be able to break down historical writing into its three central elements, narrative, analysis and description.

Section 10 Planning a history essay

You should develop the skill of planning your essays so that they communicate as clearly as possible.

1 THE VARIETY OF PRIMARY SOURCES

Remembering what was said about *primary sources* in the previous unit, in the next exercise see how many kinds of primary source you can think of. (You should do this exercise before television programme 2 *Witting and Unwitting Testimony* is broadcast, but if you have fallen behind you will find that programme very useful.)

Exercise

In your notebook list as many primary sources as you can think of. Either just list them as they occur to you or, if you feel up to it, try to organize the sources systematically into different categories. Take in the entire human past, not just the Victorian period.

Specimen answer

Documents of record

Central government sources: government edicts, laws, charters, records of exchequer, chancery and other government departments. Records of parliaments, estates or other representative institutions. Council and cabinet records, ambassadors' reports, diplomatic dispatches. Records of central law courts, central police records.

Local records: manorial records, local legal cases and reports (including, for instance, reports of the Inquisition), parish registers, local police reports, parish poor relief records, local government records, local electoral records (e.g. poll books).

Other formal records: university records, records of societies, records of political parties, trade union minutes and reports.

Private business records: estate records, wage returns, contracts, prospectuses, minutes of board meetings, and so on.

Surveys and reports

Reports of royal commissions and parliamentary committees of inquiry, Domesday Book, and so on.

Private and individual surveys: (For the Victorian period) the investigations of Henry Mayhew, reports of the Royal Statistical Society, directories and handbooks, and so on. (For the very modern period) opinion surveys, and so on.

Chronicles and histories

Monastic chronicles, 'chivalric' chronicles, town chronicles, civic histories and other contemporary histories, memoirs and autobiographies.

Family and personal sources

Letters, diaries (memoirs and autobiographies might equally well be included here).

Polemical documents and media of communication

Pamphlets, treatises and polemical writings, sermons, newspapers, cartoons, etchings and other illustrative material, posters and advertisements, films, radio tapes, television tapes.

Archaeology, industrial archaeology, history-on-the-ground, and physical artefacts

Inscriptions, entire or part remains (buildings, walls, and so on), pots and other artefacts, coins, paper money, entire or part remains of factories, old machinery, work-people's houses, remains of transportation systems, complete towns or sections of towns, furniture, old costumes, and so on.

Literary and artistic sources

Novels, romances, operas, plays, poems, philosophical writings, painting, sculpture, architecture.

Sources that are techniques as much as sources

Place names, maps, aerial photography, blood groups, statistics, processes and techniques (for example, surviving industrial processes and craftsmen at work).

'Oral history' and oral traditions (folk songs, and so on)

 Discussion

I don't for one moment suppose that you have thought of as many different varieties of primary source as that, and I certainly don't expect you to have organized your list into the sorts of category I have used. Even so, this is very far from being a complete list: without doubt one can think of many other items worthy of inclusion (and perhaps you have done so). To put the matter at its simplest, *anything* which came into existence during the particular period which the historian is studying is a primary source for that period.

Obviously, in terms of sheer practicality and utility, a line will have to be drawn somewhere. Thus the wrapping paper of a bar of chocolate will be in the strictest sense a primary source for the future historian studying the age in which we now live; on the other hand since there will be such a wealth of other primary sources we could easily forgive the future historian for ignoring the chocolate wrapper on the grounds that it is completely insignificant compared to these other sources. (However, a historian of diet, or a historian of design might well be very interested in the chocolate wrapper: in the end the value of a particular source depends on what particular topic is being investigated.)

Let me now look at each of my headings in turn. By *documents of record* I mean sources that formally record decisions whether taken by a single ruler, such as a king or emperor, or by a committee or council or parliament; in the latter case, the document may also give a formal account of the discussions and proceedings. I have made a rough, and fairly obvious distinction between records of central government, local government, and records of other institutions. Just as I have included documents relating to government business transactions as documents of record, so also I have included documents relating to private business transactions: these all are, or purport to be, records of something that definitely happened.

Then I moved on to *surveys and reports*. Such documents come into existence when a government or some other institution or individual sets out to collect information. These are of course records in a sense too, but they do not record actual decisions or transactions, but are rather the result of surveys or inquiries, or are simply collections of information.

Next came *chronicles and histories*. Of course, to qualify as primary sources these must be contemporary with the period being studied. In fact it was very common, first for monks, then later for lay commentators, to compile chronicles, or write histories of their own time. Such sources are not much used in modern history, but they are very valuable for the mediaeval period, and indeed for the Renaissance period. However, memoirs and autobiographies are very much a feature of the modern world. Autobiographies may be of leading political figures, or of course they may be entirely confined to family and personal matters.

However, on the whole I prefer to include them under this heading because autobiographies, usually written up long after the events they describe, do not have the immediacy of letters and diaries actually written at the time.

Family and personal sources could of course include the sort of business transactions I have listed separately. But as the detailed list shows, I'm thinking here of things like personal letters, private diaries and so on, which, obviously, are less a direct record of transactions or listing of information.

My next heading was the rather elaborate one of *polemical documents and media of communication*. You can see the sorts of things I have in mind, though you may be surprised that I group them all under one heading. Some historians might well use a heading here like 'artefacts of popular culture'. Now you may well think that there is a distinction between, on the one side, sermons and polemical tracts which are designed very forcefully to put one point of view, and newspapers whose basic purpose may well be the objective dissemination of information; in fact, as we all know, few if any newspapers are without some kind of axe to grind.

Archaeology, industrial archaeology, history-on-the-ground, and physical artefacts: the uses of such sources for very early periods are fairly well known. We can learn a lot about more modern periods too, particularly about lifestyles and living conditions, from, for example, household utensils, furniture and surviving buildings. Television programme 2 demonstrates some of these points, as indeed do several of the television programmes throughout the course.

Literary and artistic sources: architecture, novels, poems, paintings, sculpture, all take their place as fundamental products of the age which the historian is studying; if he does not pay attention to them, he will fail to understand that age in its total aspect. On the other hand, such creative artefacts of a past age do raise certain problems which are perhaps not always too well understood; for this reason we shall turn again to this problem in section 4.

Sources that are techniques as much as sources. That must sound very puzzling, so let me try to explain. Place names and aerial photography do not have a real physical existence dating back, say, to the Middle Ages, though they are both used as sources for mediaeval history. The taking of an aerial photograph is a *technique* for making clear the contours of a mediaeval village, say, or of prehistoric field plans which are not apparent to someone standing on the ground. To be absolutely accurate one should probably say that the actual contours of the landscape, invisible as they may be, form the real primary source, while the taking of the aerial photograph is merely a modern technique for making use of this particular source. With place names the real primary sources are old maps, charters and oral traditions from which derives our knowledge of the names. Good examples are surviving place names with such distinctively Scandinavian endings as -*by*, as in Whitby, and -*thorpe*, as in Scunthorpe, which give the historian a very good idea of the extent of Viking settlement in England. Chiswell Street, where the Whitbread Brewery founded in the eighteenth century still stood in Victorian London, *may* imply that there was once a 'choice well' there. Statistics form the most significant example of this kind of source, which is as much method as source. Certain statistics in the form of, say, pages of royal revenues, or estate accounts, or details of a country's balance of payments over several years, do have a concrete physical existence. But quite often historians extract their statistics from a wide range of different sources. What makes them *usable* is the application of statistical techniques and, usually, the employment of a computer. My final entry here may have seemed particularly obscure. But if we want to learn something, say, of village life in Victorian Britain we would find it very useful indeed if we could find a village blacksmith today still practising the craft of his ancestors. Television is particularly useful for capturing such processes and presenting them to you as students, or indeed to wider audiences.

I deliberately put 'oral history' in quotation marks because I think this title, now absorbed into everyday speech, is rather misleading. What is really meant is 'oral sources', the recording, whether on tape, by shorthand, or any other means, of personal recollections. For black Americans in the Deep South, or working-class wives in Edwardian Britain, such oral testimony is invaluable, because there is so little other source material to go on. Oral traditions (which take us back beyond living memory) are specially valuable for societies where the written word is little used.

Don't try to absorb or memorize all of this now. Rather regard this section as providing reference material to which you can turn at any time during this course, and perhaps also when you go on to other courses involving historical elements. The basic point I want to get over is the fantastic *variety* of primary sources which the historian may use and, of course, the way in which they, and not books on the shelves, form the raw material for historical study.

2 WITTING AND UNWITTING TESTIMONY

Here we come to an absolutely crucial distinction in the handling of primary sources, which is why the whole of television programme 2 is essentially concerned with it. 'Witting' means 'deliberate' or 'intentional'; 'unwitting' means 'unaware' or 'unintentional'. 'Testimony' means 'evidence'. Thus 'witting testimony' is the deliberate message of a document or other source; the 'unwitting testimony' is the unintentional evidence that it also contains. (Actually, of course, it is the writer or creator of the document or source who is intentional or unintentional, not the testimony itself, so these phrases are examples of a particular and rather effective figure of speech, known as the transferred epithet, but no need to bother with that at the moment.) Witting testimony, then, is the information that the person who originally compiled or created the document or source intended to convey.

Domesday Book came into existence because William the Conqueror wanted to know just exactly how much the land he had conquered was worth: thus he sent his investigators to every part of England to collect details of every village from the sworn testimony (a good example of the normal usage of this word!) of local men, details about who held what land and about the value of each holding and its stock. The witting testimony of Domesday Book, then, is these factual details of who owned what, how much cattle, how many sheep, what fields, and so on. But, though this was no part of William the Conqueror's intention, Domesday Book actually also gives historians fascinating insight into the structure, attitudes and life of the various communities of eleventh-century England. This is its unwitting testimony, which may well be more important to historians than the witting testimony.

Hansard's published volumes of Victorian parliamentary debates were intended to inform all interested of exactly what different ministers, ordinary MPs, had said in the House of Commons: that is their witting testimony and it is of profound interest to political historians. But this document also tells us something about the way in which parliamentary debates were conducted, about the procedures and conventions of the Victorian parliament. This is unwitting testimony, interesting, though perhaps in this case not as important as the witting testimony. However, where the basic assumptions of Members of Parliament are also revealed – for example, their almost automatic acceptance of the forms and beliefs of revealed religion, taken for granted by them, but very striking to us – then such unwitting testimony can be of great importance. Most Victorian documents do not say much about women, the clear understanding being, and this is supported wherever there are casual references to women, that women occupy an inferior place in society excluded from public life. The Victorians did not usually feel the need to express this openly (though sometimes they did); they took it for granted. But we, 'reading between the lines' as it were, that is to say reading the unwitting testimony, the unspoken assumptions, can derive a very clear impression of the role and status of women in Victorian society. Witting testimony, then, is the message a document deliberately sets out to convey to contemporaries; the unwitting testimony is evidence which historians find very useful, but which the originator of the document is not conscious is being conveyed, for it would be known anyway, or taken for granted, by contemporaries.

 Exercise

Now read the extract from the Course Reader II.3 'Horace Mann, from the Report on the Religious Census, 1851' (you have already read about the religious census of 1851 in Best, pages 196–7). Can you distinguish between Mann's witting testimony and his unwitting testimony? A very brief answer will suffice simply indicating the sorts of things that are part of Mann's deliberate message, and the sort of things he simply takes for granted.

 Specimen answer

1   Witting testimony. Mann is concerned to demonstrate that the place where religious decline was truly serious was among the working masses, and to offer an explanation for this, which he terms 'unconscious secularism'.

2   Unwitting testimony. In making these deliberate points, Mann takes it for granted that his readers will agree with his division of society into the upper classes, the middle classes, and the working masses. We have already seen how complicated the question of class is, but here is a very valuable piece of unwitting testimony suggesting a way in which people of the time saw the social structure of their society. Mann, just to drive the distinction home in case you are still puzzled, was interested in writing about religious decline and its causes (obviously with a view to reversing the process); he was not in any way concerned with writing a treatise about the class structure – it is quite apart from his own intentions that for historians looking back a clear picture of class structure is presented in his writing.

I wouldn't be at all surprised if you had difficulties with that exercise, so here is another one.

 Exercise

Read the extract from the Course Reader I.14 'Letter from S. C. Nicholson and W. H. Wood to Secretaries of Trades' Councils, Federations of Trades and Trade Societies, 16 April 1868'. Again, very briefly, distinguish the basic witting testimony from the unwitting testimony. (Note that 'Society' is just a Victorian alternative for what we would call 'Union'.)

 Specimen answer

Wittingly, the document is telling the various Labour organizations that it has been decided to hold a congress of such organizations, and is inviting representatives to attend. In this sense, the document is a document of record: it records that a decision to hold a congress has been taken; and also when the congress is to take place. The document also records the central role played by the Manchester and Salford Trades Council. More than this, the document deliberately and consciously gives reasons why this congress is necessary and why representatives should attend – for example, that there is great public ignorance about trade unions and that it seems likely that parliament will introduce legislation 'detrimental to the interests' of the unions. Perhaps the most important piece of witting testimony is the clear sense of working-class unity and determination contained in the italicized phrase.

From the *unwitting* testimony we learn that the proceedings are to be modelled on those of a very middle-class body, from which the artisan class is almost excluded, the Social Science Association, that the press is recognized as a valuable medium for ventilating the various issues (the writers clearly take this for granted, but it is of interest to us as historians), we get a clear impression of the disabilities under which unions laboured at that time (again this would be known broadly to those receiving the document; for us there are rich comparisons to be made with the situation of trade unions today), and we see that women are lumped in with children as requiring special factory legislation.

I hope you are now beginning to see what I am getting at. If you are still hopelessly puzzled you must read through this section again, but if you do see broadly what I am on about, continue through the unit where the nature of witting and unwitting testimony will become clearer and clearer. But before that, just one final exercise.

 Exercise

Imagine you are writing a historical study of 'The Founding of the Open University and its Impact on Higher Education in Britain in the early 1970s'. Note down the sorts of source materials you would use, and indicate which sources you think would be important mainly for witting testimony and those which would be important mainly for unwitting testimony.

Specimen answer and discussion

1   The parliamentary debates, political announcements, and other documents relating to the founding of the Open University, such as the Open University Charter. This would mainly be witting testimony establishing the actual record as to when the idea was put forward, and when the University actually was founded.

2   Internal Open University documents, recording discussions and decisions on educational matters, course team discussions, and so on, together with the course materials (for example, the original Arts Foundation course A100). There would be witting testimony on decisions, but also much unwitting testimony about the educational attitudes and assumptions of Open University staff. Course material offers a marvellous example of the distinction between witting and unwitting testimony. My witting purpose in writing these units is to help you to learn the basic principles of historical study. Unwittingly I am probably giving away all sorts of information about my own assumptions and prejudices. Think what a future historian might do with that!

3   Materials from other universities and colleges, articles in the press, and so on, giving evidence of the Open University's impact. Articles explicitly describing the Open University's influence would be mainly witting testimony. But if, say, one came across a history lecture syllabus from another university which went on and on about witting testimony and unwitting testimony, though without any acknowledgement of or reference to the *Introduction to History* in the original A100 – then this would be unwitting testimony that, whether acknowledged or not, these original Open University units had had an impact on history teaching at another university!

4   Accounts and autobiographies written by members of the Open University staff, for example, the account written by Lord Perry, the Open University's original Vice-Chancellor. One would expect such material to contain clear factual information (witting testimony), but again insights into the attitudes and motives of the early founders of the Open University (mainly unwitting testimony).

3 CRITICISM AND EVALUATION OF PRIMARY SOURCES

In defining 'research' I stressed that as well as the all-important work in primary sources, it also involved the reading of all relevant secondary sources. The fact is that when historians come to evaluate and interpret primary documents they already have a deep knowledge of their chosen period of study, and this knowledge is invaluable to them in interpreting primary documents. Thus there is something slightly artificial in presenting you with documents when, inevitably, you have little general historical knowledge, though since I am choosing my examples from Victorian Britain you will be able to make some use of your reading of Best. Anyway, even if the exercises are somewhat abstract, my main purpose is to get over the basic elementary principles of source criticism.

Here I am going to set out in rather schematic form the questions which have to be asked of any primary source, though in practice professional historians will deal with many of these questions instinctively without having to work through them systematically, and in many cases will already know the answers to some of the questions. Still, I want you to be aware explicitly of the activities which, consciously or unconsciously, historians must undertake in making use of primary sources.

Theoretically, the first point a historian must establish about any primary source is its *authenticity*. That is he or she must establish that the document really is what it purports to be; that, say, a tract purporting to be written by Luther really was written by Luther, not by an imitator or a detractor, or that a charter issued by the French King Henry IV to the town of Rouen really was issued by Henry IV, not forged later, say, by the citizens of the town wishing to create special privileges for themselves, or that the diaries of Gladstone really were written by Gladstone and not, say, fabricated and then 'discovered' by one of his biographers. The biography of the Victorian novelist Thomas Hardy, *The Life of Thomas Hardy,* by his second wife provides an interesting case in point. Scholars subsequently established that the biography had in fact been written by Hardy himself, which, of course, changes its whole nature as evidence. As a relatively objective, factual account by a woman who knew him only in later life it is not *authentic*; in fact it contains the modified version of events which Hardy wished to convey to posterity. On the other hand, as an autobiography by Hardy himself it is authentic, and where compared with the real facts as we know them, gives interesting insights into Hardy's thought processes.

However, most of the documents that working historians use are well vouched for; it is only occasionally that a new document is discovered where strict tests for authenticity have to be carried out. So, for the purposes of this foundation course, we shall take it that all the documents that you are studying have had their authenticity fully established.

Taking authenticity as established, there are then a series of basic questions which historians, explicitly or implicitly, must ask of every source they have to deal with.

1   What date is it? How close is its date to the date of the events described? And where several documents are being analysed together, as is normal in most serious historical study, where does the date of this particular document fit in with the dates of the other documents? What, in short, is the significance of the date? Some documents and, of course, visual sources, buildings and physical artefacts raise considerable problems of dating; but all of the documents you will be dealing with will be firmly dated.

2   What type of source is it? A private letter? Or an official report, or what?

3   How did the source come into existence in the first place, and for what purpose? What person, or group of persons, created the source? What basic

attitudes, prejudices, vested interests would he, she or they be likely to have? For example, Protestant writers in the Victorian period describing the revival of Catholicism could not always be expected to be completely objective. For whom is the document intended, to whom is it addressed? The Conservative Prime Minister Disraeli always wrote very ingratiatingly to Queen Victoria; this did not always help his accuracy. Thus knowledge of the social position or social class of the originator of a document, and often of the recipient as well, should be established.

4   How far is the author of the source really in a good position to provide reliable information on the particular topic the historian is interested in? Disraeli wrote a novel called *Sybil*, sub-titled 'The Two Nations', the rich and the poor: how far was he really in a position to understand the lives of the poor? How far was Marx in a position to understand the British working class? We know that his associate, Friedrich Engels, though a very wealthy businessman, did have first-hand knowledge of the Manchester slums, through his Irish-born girlfriend. If we read a newspaper account of the Sheffield strikes of 1868, we want to be sure, at the very least, that the reporter was actually there, and is not depending simply on hearsay.

5   What did the document mean to contemporaries? Though of course the historian will go on to draw out from the document conclusions which contemporaries were not aware of, before he can even begin to approach the document he must first be sure that he understands it as contemporaries understood it, and this, naturally, can only be achieved by someone who already has a very deep knowledge of the period. However, there are specific sub-questions which you can note:

(a)   There's the problem of deciphering inscriptions, hieroglyphics and certain types of handwriting (even just plain bad handwriting). We won't inflict any of these problems on you.

(b)   There are the problems of archaic or foreign languages. Again, you will scarcely be involved in this, though you will find that the Victorians wrote in a style that is not quite the same as our own, and sometimes used words in slightly different ways. It is, to repeat, part of the historian's skill to understand Victorian language as the Victorians understood it.

(c)   Apart from the general language problem, there is the problem of specific technical or semi-technical phrases. Thus in the trade union document we have just analysed, we have to know that 'Society' means a 'Trade Society', that is to say a 'Trade Union'.

(d)   There are problems of references and allusions in the document. Again to make full use of that trade union document we have to know something about the Social Science Association. If any names or places are referred to, we have to know who the people are, we have to know the location and significance of the places.

6   There is a last question which is generally, though not exclusively, of relevance to archaeological sources and artefacts, rather than to written sources: where was the source found? But for the purposes of your study you can ignore this question.

The purpose of applying all of these critical questions to the document is to serve as a preliminary to asking the really important question: 'What does the document tell us?' What it tells, both in the form of witting and unwitting testimony, will in large part depend upon what questions are asked, what particular problem or subject the historian is addressing.

 Exercise

Turn to the extract from the Course Reader 1.7 'Report of Leonard Horner, Factory Inspector, to Lord Palmerston, Home Secretary, 1852'. Read the first two sentences of the report and the last paragraph. What general impression do you derive of the state of the economy in 1852? Reading the rest of the paragraph, what reactions do you have?

Specimen answer and discussion

Clearly, there is a great sense of boom and optimism. But in the third sentence Horner unwittingly gives us quite a striking insight into Victorian attitudes which might come as something of a shock to us today: he is perfectly happy about children working half-time in the factories.

This document really does give a marvellous impression of the duality of Victorian society: the prosperity and optimism built on the hard work, and often misery, of the masses, including children. For evidence that rather contradicts Homer (though it does come a little earlier) you could look at the extract in the Course Reader 1.6 (a), where a London costermonger is commenting on how little money the working classes have to spend.

 Exercise

Turn to the extract from the Course Reader V.3 'Speech by Thomas Babington Macaulay at Edinburgh, 2 November 1852'. List the questions that you would have to ask of this document before going on to decide what the document tells you; if you can think of any answers to these questions, however hesitant, put them down too. Then, imagining that you are researching on 'Mid-Victorian attitudes' note down what the document tells you, distinguishing between the witting and the unwitting testimony.

 Specimen answer

1   What date is it? Has its date any special significance? Well, the date is 1852, four years after the European revolutions of 1848 ('the madness of 1848'). Most significantly, we are well into the beginning of the great mid-Victorian boom of which you have already heard so much; in fact, a year after the Great Exhibition which celebrated Victorian optimisim and prosperity.

2   What type of source is it? You're told the answer to that one: it is a speech. A historian of the period would know (though I can't expect you to know this) that Macaulay had been MP for Edinburgh from 1839–47, and that in fact he won his seat again in this very year, 1852: so this is a political speech by an MP to his constituents.

3   Who created the source? For what purpose? What biases might we expect? And so on. In fact, we need to know about Macaulay's social position and social background. Again, let me add details which, of course, I couldn't possibly expect you to know. His father was a merchant, sponsoring trading ventures to such places as Sierra Leone. To begin with the family were prosperous enough for Macaulay to be able to go to Trinity College, Cambridge. But, as his father's ventures failed, Macaulay largely created his own fortune, partly from his immensely successful historical writing, partly from well-paid government posts. He was a Whig politician and minister, and became a peer five years after this speech. Personally I would regard him as a newly-arrived member of the mid-Victorian upper class (Macaulay is, in my view, one of very many examples of individuals who simply do not fit classical Marxist analysis). Anyway, it would be generally agreed that Macaulay's are the views of the wealthiest and most powerful political connection of the time, the Whigs. His views will have all the prejudices of that particular group of people.

4   Is the author of the source in a good position to provide reliable information? Well, presumably Macaulay will not tell us about *all* mid-Victorian attitudes, but he would seem to be an ideal source for telling us about Whig attitudes. And, in so far as he was a highly popular and successful historian, one might accept him as the proponent of widely acceptable ideas.

5   What did the document mean to contemporaries? What particular problems of interpretation are there? The best way of dealing with these questions is to work through the document explaining any phrases that need explaining. 'The madness of 1848': contemporaries would still be very aware of the upheavals

in Europe in 1848 'Ten plagues', 'land of Goshen': unless you are particularly well versed in the Bible (as, of course, Victorian readers were) you would (like me!) have to look this up — the reference is to Exodus 8:22 and 9:26, Goshen being the district in Ancient Egypt, protected from the plagues raging all around, where the Israelites were. The Habeas Corpus Act, as you may know, is the act that prevents anyone being imprisoned without trial. Sir Robert Peel, now dead ('beyond the reach of envy'), son of an immensely rich cotton manufacturer and himself also in effect a member of the upper class, was the Conservative leader who repealed the Corn Laws thus establishing almost total free trade ('the great commercial reform of 1846'), in so doing breaking with the mainstream of the Conservative or Tory party so that his followers were eventually to join with the Whigs. Lord John Russell belonged to one of the most powerful of all the aristocratic Whig families.

Now, what does the document tell us about 'Victorian attitudes'? *Wittingly* the document states that Britain escaped revolution in 1848 because of 'a wise and noble constitution', capable of responding to 'force of reason and public opinion' with reforms, the two crucial ones being the repeal of the Corn Laws and the Reform Act of 1832. At the same time it is recognized that the constitution is not perfect, it needs to be purified and amended. Above all the message is that of the necessity to avoid extremes. In short, this is an excellent statement of Whig principles, the principles of the dominant group in Victorian society. The emphasis on 'law and order' is particularly striking.

The *unwitting* testimony simply reinforces the witting. Macaulay takes it for granted that the European revolutions were 'madness', that the highly unequal and undemocratic system of 1852 could be described as 'British liberty', and that the British people enjoyed a 'singular happiness'. The reference to Goshen, of course, points up once again the importance of revealed religion.

So, remembering that Macaulay is making a political speech supporting Whig ideas of moderate reform, we do get from this document a very clear insight into the political attitudes which dominated the 1850s – the weight is very much on maintaining things as they are rather than on any particular changes.

 Cassette exercise

Cassette 2, side 1, band 2 contains a substantial exercise, and you should be prepared to spend at least an hour on it. Before listening to the cassette you should read the relevant section in the Cassette Notes.

4 LITERATURE AND ART AS PRIMARY SOURCES

The use of literature and art as historical sources raises problems which are not always fully recognized.

One obvious point must be stressed at the outset. A novel or a poem is a source for the period *in* which it was written, not for the period *about* which it was written. In other words the novels of Sir Walter Scott may tell us a good deal about the early nineteenth century when Scott himself was writing; but though Scott was undoubtedly historically minded, his historical novels do not generally give us serious information about the ages in which they are supposed to be set. They may tell us a little through the author's own imaginative historical insight — so that in this sense they become a kind of popularized secondary source — but they certainly are not primary sources for these ages. In the same way a Renaissance painting of the Crucifixion will be a marvellous primary source for the Renaissance, but it will in no sense be a primary source for the first century AD. Shakespeare's history plays are good sources for contemporary attitudes towards politics and society and, in particular, for Tudor attitudes to English history: they are not, obviously, primary sources for the historical Macbeth, Hamlet or Richard II.

Too ready use has sometimes been made of novels in the writing of that species of 'social history' sometimes more appropriately referred to as 'polite chat about the past'. Art and literature, being an important facet of the age that produced them, must always rank as important primary sources for the study of that age. But it is misusing literature to expect to find in it the concrete facts of everyday existence, wage rates, living standards, environmental conditions, and so on. For information on these matters the historian should prefer not to take the word of the novelist (whose first concern after all is not with providing an exact factual record of physical conditions), but should instead turn to various of the other types of primary sources already mentioned: government papers, statistical series, company records, trade union archives, private correspondence, or various forms of archaeological remains. A painting or etching (or other form of visual art) *may* provide reliable information on what a particular environment looked like at a particular time — for instance, much of our knowledge of what seventeenth-century London looked like is derived in this way. But the historian must always remember that the painter may have been affected by prevailing stylistic conventions, or by his own artistic purposes, so that the painting is very far from being an exact factual record.

What the historian can usefully derive from imaginative literature is an insight into social *attitudes*, particularly attitudes towards that great problem, *social status and social class*, and also attitudes towards matters of *belief* and *prejudice* (is the monarchy felt to be divine, is travelling on Sunday held to be sinful, and so on).

To gain this insight, the historian will, of course, have to saturate himself or herself in the literature of the period: it is not good enough to lift a couple of easy quotations out of one or two novels, which may in fact turn out to be highly unrepresentative. Something of this perception, too, may be derived from visual art. It is, for instance, very striking that mediaeval artists tended to present peasants and craftsmen as if smaller in physical size than kings and great lords.

A value to the historian provided by both art and literature is that they may suggest to him clues which he *ought to follow up* in other types of source. If he finds a statement or a description in a novel or a poem, or some piece of illustration in a painting, which does not seem to him to accord with the generally accepted picture of the age which he is studying, he will not immediately decide that this generally accepted picture must be overthrown. But on the other hand he will at least try to check from his other sources whether in fact there is any validity in the discrepancy which he has detected in his literary or artistic source.

The great danger which must always be guarded against in handling art and literature in historical study is that of presenting a too simple notion of art and literature 'reflecting' a particular age. More will be said about this later. But you might for the moment ponder over the danger that this notion that art and literature 'reflect' a particular age can simply degenerate into a circular argument. First of all the age is defined, say, as the 'Elizabethan Age' or the 'Victorian Age': certain characteristics are attributed to these ages, most of them drawn anyway from the art and literature of this age; then the art and literature are studied more systematically, when, lo and behold, the characteristics which have already been predetermined in the mind of the writer are discovered in the art and literature, and said to reflect their particular age.

Figure 1

This is by the way of being a warning, not an absolute embargo. Of course there is a very real relationship between the historical and social context and the art and literature of the age. It is one of the tasks of the historian to explore this relationship. But you must always be on your guard against any simple use of art and literature as a 'mirror of the age' or as revealing 'the climate of the age' or whatever other question-begging cliché you care to use.

When you come to study *Hard Times* you will find much fruitful interaction between history and literature, and that is something we very much want to encourage – but do keep the obvious dangers in mind. In studying a novel as a primary historical source we ask the same questions we would ask about any source, but I would particularly like to place emphasis on:

1   What date is it, and how does that date relate to the period which is actually being written about?

2   Did the author have first-hand experience of the events and circumstances being described? Or is the author at least drawing upon childhood memories, or upon recollections passed on by his family.

Exercise

What questions of dating have to be settled before one could use *Hard Times* as a primary source? On the basis of the answers, how reliable would you regard *Hard Times* as a historical source?

 Specimen answer and discussion

When was it written? What period of time was it written about? You don't have to look very far to find that it was published in 1854, and if you glance at the introduction you'll find that it was still being written in 1854; the same introduction, which refers to Dickens's report on the Preston lock-out of 1854, suggests that Dickens was broadly writing about the late 1840s and early 1850s. From the point of view of dating, then, this should be a particularly reliable historical source. But, as always, we have to remember that a novel is a work of creative imagination: it is not Dickens's primary purpose to give us factual information, so we shall need to be on our guard against taking what seems like social description, or factual information, as necessarily historically completely accurate.

 Exercise

I want you now to read or re-read Chapters 10 and 11 of the first book of *Hard Times*. In common with much of the rest of the book these two chapters appear to contain pieces of information relating to the main points about Victorian society that have already been made. But given that this is a work of fiction, and given that Dickens had certain clear literary and moral purposes, some of these pieces of information are likely to be more reliable than others. I am going to set out a list of headings relating to the points of potential interest to historians (whether they are reliable or accurate or not) made in the course of these two chapters. I want you to note down the information that relates to each heading, and I want you to comment on how reliable or accurate you feel that information to be, giving reasons if you can. In connection with the heading 'Class and class relationships' there is one piece of information I'd particularly like you to be sure to note, and I'd like you to try to comment upon its significance and place it in its historical context: this is where Mr Bounderby refers to Stephen Blackpool by his first name. Do you, for instance, take this to be a sign of informal friendliness?

Here are the headings:

1   Social conditions in an industrial town
2   Class and class relationships
3   Factory life
4   Working-class dress
5   Role and customs of the undertaker
6   Moral standards (two or three points to be made here)
7   Employers' eating habits

 Specimen answer and discussion

1   The second paragraph gives a very powerful description of narrow, suffocating streets and courts. But this is a highly dramatic description. I'd say it's not very useful for getting a really accurate picture of social conditions.

2   Workers are known dismissively as 'Hands'. On a brief point of clear fact a novelist would be much less likely to be inventive. The usage anyway has lasted into the twentieth century (and we find it in other sources including Dickens's article on the Preston strike, extract IV.6 in the Course Reader). This is reliable in indicating the dismissive attitude of the employing middle or upper class towards the working class. From the opening, and from the second last paragraph on the working class has its own quarter separate from the hill on which the middle

class lives. This would seem to be accurate enough; such geographical class divisions are fairly common. Now we come to the bit where Bounderby addresses Blackpool as 'Stephen'. I am sure you deduced that this was hardly informal friendliness, but I would scarcely expect you to know that it is a continuance of a pre-industrial tradition when those at the bottom of the social scale were known only by a christian name, with those above that being referred to as Goodman so-and-so, and only the group above that being called Mr or Master (if you glance on to the bottom of page 102, about a third of the way down the page, you will find Dickens using both the word of industrial society, 'class', and the word of pre-industrial society, 'order', within the space of a few words in the same sentence). Stephen is very respectful, though not servile towards his employer; we gather that other workers are rather more aggressive towards their employers. I would not expect you to note this, but it is significant that chapter 11 is entitled 'No Way Out': there is a great deal of documentation and literature of all kinds to suggest that a fundamental characteristic of working-class life is of it being a kind of life sentence from which there is no escape (the idea is even repeated in the revolutionary film of the 1950s, *Room at the Top*).

3   We learn that bells are rung at clocking-on time and knocking-off time, and that the workers get an hour for lunch. These sound like the little touches of local detail which a novelist would wish to put in and there is no reason to doubt their accuracy. There is also a more imaginative description of what Stephen feels in his own head when the machinery stops. That's a nice touch which a historian might be very glad to pick up, though it can scarcely be regarded as a reliable comment on factory life in general.

4   We learn of the shawls of the women workers and of Blackpool's loose neckerchief. There is no reason at all to doubt the accuracy of these details.

5   We learn that funerals are the only occasions for a show of pomp in the neighbourhood, and that the undertaker does well out of them. This seems to serve no special moral purpose and would seem to be accurate. The references to the black ladder are fascinating and again ring true: it is difficult to imagine Dickens inventing this out of nothing. This reference could actually be added to my first heading since it does in a very potent way bring home the meanness of the industrial environment.

6   In reference to Blackpool's alcoholic wife, Dickens speaks of 'foul moral infamy'. Here even he seems to be joining in the widespread Victorian censorious moral tone. We then learn about the prevailing attitudes towards marriage and divorce (only open to the very rich). It was vital for Dickens to be accurate here, or his plot would not have carried conviction with his readers, thus we can take this as reliable. One might also note the sexual innocence of the relationship between Blackpool and Rachel – this would seem to be in keeping with the standards of Respectability stressed by Best.

7   We have to be a little careful: 'chop and sherry' is a rather neat phrase, and anyway Dickens is always describing people eating chops. No doubt the contrast that is intended is with Blackpool's 'nothing but a little bread'. Still, dietary information is not always easy to come by, and historians in this sphere do have to make great use of imaginative literature. (Also, of course, books of household management – see the extract from the Course Reader IV.9 'Mrs Isabella Beeton, from *Beeton's Book of Household Management, 1859-61*'.)

 Exercise

Best makes very frequent use of literature. Towards the end of Unit 1, section 7, I was rather critical of Best's use of a long quotation on page 196 from Dickens's report from Edinburgh. As you read through Best, decide for yourself where you feel he makes legitimate use of literature as a historical source and where you feel his use is less desirable.

Now read pages 263 and 264 of Best. It seems to me that here he goes out of his way to be very careful and genuinely historical in his use of literary references. In what way does this careful, cautious approach show itself?

 Specimen answer

He makes it clear that the view of class in *Little Dorrit* is 'highly coloured', and on the next page he says of Matthew Arnold's 'highly coloured picture' that it is 'at least as much of a caricature as Dickens's'. So here, at least, Best is using literature to point up certain features, while recognizing that novelists often exaggerate.

5 THE IMPERFECT AND FRAGMENTARY NATURE OF HISTORICAL SOURCES

If you have followed the material presented in this unit you should now be aware that the historian's task is by no means an easy one. The difficulties we have discussed could be summarized under two headings: (1) the immense range and variety of the sources that historians must be prepared to make use of; and (2) the complicated critical techniques that they have to bring to bear on these sources once they have found them. But this does not really complete the picture. You may feel that once the sources have been discovered, once authenticity has been established, and once the various biases have been allowed for and the various technical problems resolved, then it is fairly plain sailing towards producing a reasonable reconstruction of whatever aspect of the past the particular historian is interested in; but this is not necessarily so, since however dedicated and skilful the historian, nothing can compensate for the fact that most of the sources bequeathed to us by past ages are fragmentary, incomplete or simply not relevant to the questions historians wish to answer.

In the next unit I shall turn specifically to the question of controversy in historical writing, that is, the manner in which disagreement arises among the most distinguished and hard-working historians over their interpretation of past events. We have already noted possible reasons for this, in particular the unavoidable subjective element in history and the extent to which theory is or is not felt to be applicable. But it must be stressed that even if by some miracle the subjective element could be wished away, historians would still find themselves in disagreement. Even if their methods could become much more purely scientific, the very fact that the evidence is so imperfect and fragmentary would still leave much scope for controversy.

The problem is at its most obvious in the more distant periods of study. Archaeological digs rarely uncover anything like complete physical artefacts. Mediaeval documents were frequently burnt or otherwise destroyed. But though there may be, in quantity, masses of material for the study of Victorian Britain, and even more for later periods, this material is not necessarily always suitable for the precise purposes of the historian. As we have seen, documents come into existence to serve the purposes of the people of the time, and these people are usually not the least bit interested in the sorts of issues that preoccupy later historians.

 Exercise

We have already had an example of the way in which an important issue relating to mid-Victorian Britain could not be settled because the evidence is not sufficiently conclusive. What was that?

Specimen answer

I was thinking of the question of whether wage rates were or were not going up in the 1850s, discussed by Best. But you might have referred to the question of class and social structure, such a subtle and complex topic that it is really quite difficult to imagine what sorts of documents and other evidence would be needed to give an absolutely conclusive picture of class in Victorian society.

Whatever different problems historians of different eras and different societies encounter, there always comes a point when a historian has to *squeeze the last drop* of information out of the evidence. This is a good image, and worth remembering.

 Exercise

Read these passages from historical works, both concerned with rather remote periods of London history; *A* with fourth-century Roman London, *B* with tenth- and eleventh-century Saxon London. Indicate which passage you think recognizes more realistically the fragmentary nature of historical sources.

Passage A

Across the Thames, a little further downstream than the present London Bridge, was a wooden bridge, wide enough to carry two streams of traffic, one leaving Londinium for the transriverine suburb, whose site now lies buried beneath the streets of Southwark; the other stream entering the city through the gate whose towers looked down upon the square-rigged ships moored at the long wharfs below.

Inside the walls the paved main streets of the city's centre were wide and straight and regular, the buildings that lined them solid and imposing. Although the labourers and the men who worked on the docks still lived in little huts like beehives or in wooden houses with thatched or shingle roofs, much of the Roman reconstruction that had followed the devastation of the city by Boadicea had been carried out in brick, stone and tile. Most buildings, their walls painted a dark red, their low-pitched roofs a lighter, salmon colour, were small and low; but there were others, it seems, four or even five storeys high with fountains playing in their courtyards and vines growing against their garden walls.

The Basilica, centre of commerce and government, which faced the traveller as he entered the city through the river gate, was a vast and impressive building on Cornhill, five hundred feet long, whose arcaded walls, lined inside with marble, were about seventy feet high; while the temple dedicated to the mysterious Mithras, the Persian god of light whose cult had been adopted by the Legions, was as graceful as any to be found in the western provinces of the Empire.

Passage B

The pre-Norman bridge of London is first mentioned, by chance, in a charter of the reign of the Saxon King Edgar (AD 959–75), in connection with a woman deliberately drowned as a witch for pin-sticking: *adrencte hir aet Lundenebridgce*. Other Saxon references to the bridge occur during the reigns of Ethelred II (978–1016) and his eldest son, Edmund Ironside (1016). The name of the former is specially closely connected with the bridge in several ways. In his fourth code of laws, which is concerned only with London (*De Institutis de Lundonie*), it is laid down that toll was to be paid for vessels coming to the bridge with fish: a halfpenny was due from a small ship and a penny from a larger one. During these two reigns the second wave of Viking invasion was at its height, and it is recorded in the *Anglo-Saxon Chronicle* under the year 1013 that when Swein Forkbeard, King of Denmark, who had marched from Winchester, was about to besiege London many of his men were drowned in the Thames 'because they kept not to the bridge'. Two years later, in 1015, there is a description of the bridge and of a fight for it in *St Olaf's Saga*, written in the thirteenth century in praise of Olaf Haroldson, the Christian king of the Norwegians, who died in 1030 and was rapidly accepted as a saint. This stirring tale of the bridge is not regarded in the contemporary *Anglo-Saxon Chronicle* but its essential elements are probably true.

... Some years ago, at the turn of last century, several weapons and tools were found lying together in the alluvium of the former foreshore of the Thames not far from the north end of the late Norman bridge of London. The implements included battle axes, spearheads, a grappling iron, a woodman's axe and a pair of tongs. As they would seem to be part of the equipment of a Viking warship, and can be dated as not much later than AD 1000, it is probable that they are associated with the Viking attacks detailed above on the old Saxon timber bridge, the site of which will be considered later.

Specimen answer and discussion

A's description of Roman London is just too smooth and self-confident, given that the main sources are archaeological. *B* recognizes much more openly the nature of the various types of source from which information can be squeezed. Note that we are not concerned with the quality of these passages as *historical communication* (a vitally important aspect to be discussed in the next unit). Passage *B* certainly is too disjointed to rank as good historical writing. But that is not the point at issue here.

Exercise

Here are some photographs of fragmentary or difficult historical sources. Say what you think each is, comment on the difficulties in using it, and suggest what positive uses could be made of it by the historian.

Figure 2

Figure 3

Figure 4

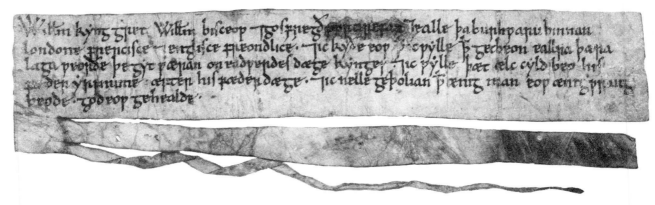

Figure 5

 Specimen answers

Figure 2 This is a pot or vessel, used probably for oil, or perhaps wine. Although we have only a part, there is enough to suggest the general shape and dimensions of the pot. Obviously before we can make use of this source, we have to ask the usual questions: how did it come into existence, and so on. For this sort of source, we would also need to know where it was found. Needless to say, I do not expect you to have any full answers to these questions, but I hope that your mind was beginning to move in the right direction. Certainly, the pot must tell us something about the domestic lifestyle of the people who used it. You should have got that relatively simple point. But, in fact, for the expert even this fragment of evidence can reveal a great deal more. Archaeologists can attribute its origins to the East Mediterranean; since it was found in London, in a layer of soil which archaeologists believe to have been deposited after the fifth century, this fragment can be taken as evidence that trade continued between the East Mediterranean and London after the fifth century.

Figure 3 This is not an easy one to make out. In fact it is the remains of a Roman ship. Again, even from these fragments, we can build up a picture of the entire ship. We can also, in the background to the left, discern the cargo of stone. To tell more than this, the evidence has to be fitted into the broader contexts in exactly the same way as with the fragment of pot.

Figure 4 Again, just by looking at this, you can see the problems of interpretation. These are in fact notes and sketches by one of the great figures of the Italian Renaissance, Leonardo Da Vinci. As you may know, he made these notes in 'mirror writing'. However, once the technique of interpreting them has been mastered, obviously they are an absolutely first class source for the ideas and thoughts of this very important Renaissance figure.

Figure 5 What is immediately striking about this charter is its extreme brevity. You can see clearly what the original Anglo-Saxon looks like, and grasp immediately some of the problems of translation. Even in translation, there remain many of the sorts of technical problems we have already discussed. However, as a charter this is a document of record (it is in fact William the Conqueror's Charter to the City of London) and must therefore tell us something substantial and concrete.

You may feel all that has taken you rather too far away from Victorian Britain. But for Victorian Britain the principle is the same. However much evidence there may seem to be, it is never neatly cut-and-dried and ready to yield straightforward answers to the questions historians want to ask. An important topic is that introduced by Professor Best on his first page, the advent of what he calls 'the relative gloom of the so-called Great Depression'. Now you might think this would be simple enough: economic boom, prosperity and social harmony in the mid-Victorian period from 1850–73, then economic depression. But in fact economic sources are particularly hard to interpret (think of the great difficulties our politicians have today in understanding what's happening to the economy), and many historians have recently argued that there was really no such thing as a Great Depression (note that Best says 'so-called') and that by all the important economic indicators Britain went on prospering and being economically successful.

You would expect there to be plenty of straightforward material on Gladstone and Disraeli and on the major decisions of government. But in the Victorian period no formal Cabinet records were kept: all we have are the letters that the prime minister wrote to Queen Victoria reporting on what had happened at Cabinet meetings. These, obviously, are partial, limited and indeed fragmentary sources. And things do not necessarily get all that better once proper Cabinet records started being taken during the First World War.

 Exercise

Turn to the extract from the Course Reader V.10 'Letter from William Ewart Gladstone to Queen Victoria, 25 February 1886', reporting on Cabinet discussions.

1   Comment on the imperfections and inadequacies of this document as a source for Cabinet discussions and decisions.

2   Nevertheless the document does tell us about some important developments and about the attitudes of Liberal ministers at the time. Note briefly what you learn from the document.

 Specimen answers

1   The report is extremely brief, with only a few lines on each of four issues. We get no idea at all of what different points of view were put forward, and by whom. The two sentences on the Crofter's Bill, in particular, tell us practically nothing.

2   However, it is interesting to learn that a Women's Suffrage Bill is coming before parliament. We could learn that from other sources, of course, but this letter reveals that ministers are both against it and unwilling, as a government, to oppose it openly: as Liberals they prefer to have the matter treated as an open question. As with the Crofter's Bill, we need much more information before we can make much of the Sir D. Wolff mission. But the evidence of growing expenditure by Army and Navy at a time of imperial expansion is significant; we should also note the paradox of Liberal reluctance to see military expenditure increase and their powerlessness to do anything about it.

Even the most fragmentary documents will usually yield something if approached in the right way; but from this section I want you to grasp above all the difficulties historians have in getting clear, unambiguous answers from their sources.

6 COMMUNICATION

The practice of history involves four basic activities.

1   The historian must go out and find source materials.

2   He must bring to bear on them the critical techniques I have just been discussing, and the knowledge he already has of the period and topic he is studying.

3   Out of this interaction he must produce an *interpretation*, his version of events and relationships between events, including, as relevant, his explanation of *why* people did what they did.

4   Finally, he must *communicate* this interpretation to his audience.

As a student you too will go through these activities, though of course your sources will (I hope!) not be too hard to find, and your interpretations will not quite be of the same character as those of a historical scholar. But if you are to be a good student of history and, indeed, of the arts, you must be able to communicate.

Even if the professional historian has made marvellous new discoveries in primary source material which no one else has ever seen, he has not completed his job if these discoveries remain buried in his own head, and are never communicated to anyone else. The audience to which the historian communicates may be small (other specialist historians) or large (the entire reading public); but whatever audience he is communicating with, the historian must present his findings in a proper and acceptable fashion.

The communication will be in the form of a book, or article, or perhaps a lecture or a radio talk. Once written, such books and articles form what we have already described as secondary sources. Put in a different way, the final task of the historian can be described as the conversion of the 'raw material' of the primary source into the finished product, the secondary source – still a 'source' in the sense that this finished product will be the main source of information for students and the general reader, people who do not have the time or the ability to search all the primary sources every time they want a particular bit of historical information.

Later in this course you will have to present your findings, in history, in literature, and so on, and in interdisciplinary work in the form of a properly written essay. If we now study the way in which basic information derived from the sources is turned into properly written history, this should both contribute to your understanding of the nature of history as a discipline, and to your skill in writing essays in all of the arts subjects.

 Exercise

For the purposes of this exercise we have to make the utterly unreal assumption that you are one of the first to research on the life of the Victorian intellectual John Stuart Mill, and that not much is yet known about his life (in fact there are shelves groaning with books on J. S. Mill).

Imagine, then, that you are a pioneer researcher on John Stuart Mill and from his *Letters*, his *Autobiography*, his published treatises, the memoirs of his contemporaries, and newspaper accounts, you have discovered the following:

1   Among his published treatises with dates of publication are (there are many others, but we'll ignore them in order to keep this exercise manageable):
Principles of Political Economy, 1848 (shows some sympathy for aspirations of working class, see the extract from the Course Reader III.10(b)); *On Liberty,* 1859 (the classic exposition of Liberal principles); and *The Subjection of Women,* 1869 (advocates political equality for women).

2   1865 elected to Parliament as Radical Liberal MP for Westminster, having made conditions that he would neither spend money nor canvass for votes, and that he must be free from considering only the purely local interests of his constituents.

3   In 1830 he meets Mrs Harriet Taylor (aged 22), the wife of John Taylor, a prosperous London merchant.

4   He was born in London, 1806, eldest son of the Scottish philosopher, historian and senior administrator in the East India Company's London office, James Mill.

5   1809–20 educated at home by his father, starting Greek at the age of three, learning also Latin, Chemistry and the Differential Calculus before he was twelve.

60

6   1823 arrested but not imprisoned for distributing birth-control propaganda.

7   1831–40 publishes many essays showing interest in both Romantic Poetry (particularly Coleridge and Wordsworth) and Political Radicalism.

8   Has a mental breakdown during the winter of 1826–7.

9   1836 severe illness following death of his father.

10   1854 severe illness.

11   1823 first job as clerk in East India Company's London office.

12   After a previous promotion, in 1856 achieves same senior post his father had held.

13   1858 government takes over administration of East India Company: being against government control of private enterprise, Mill resigns.

14   1868 loses his seat in Parliament.

15   1849 John Taylor dies.

16   Between 1830 and 1849 Mill had dined with Mrs Taylor two or three times a week (her husband dining at his club). He and Mrs Taylor travelled frequently together in England and on the Continent.

17   1851 Mill marries Harriet Taylor.

18   1854 starts writing his *Autobiography*, finally revised in 1870, and published in 1873.

19   1858 Harriet dies.

20   1873 Mill dies.

21   During discussions of Reform Bill in parliament, 1867, Mill tries unsuccessfully to have votes for women included.

22   In 1854 when Harriet was abroad, Mill wrote to her about the *Autobiography* he was then working on:

> ... a full writing out as far as anything can write out, what you are, as far as I am competent to describe you, and what I owe to you – but, besides that until revised by you it is little better than unwritten, it contains nothing about our private circumstances, further than shewing that there was intimate friendship for many years, and you only can decide what more it is necessary or desirable to say in order to stop the mouths of enemies hereafter ... will you not my own love in one of your sweetest letters give me your general notion of what we should say or imply respecting our private concerns. As it is, it shews confidential friendship and strong attachment ending in marriage when you were free and ignores there having ever been any scandalous suspicions about us ...

23   In the *Autobiography* as published, this passage appears:

> I ... was greatly indebted to the strength of character which enabled her to disregard the false interpretations liable to be put on the frequency of my visits to her while living generally apart from Mr Taylor, and on our occasionally travelling together, though in all other respects our conduct during those years gave not the slightest ground for any other supposition than the true one, that our relation to each other at that time was of strong affection and confidential intimacy only. For though we did not consider the ordinances of society binding on a subject so entirely personal, we did feel bound that our conduct should be such as in no degree to bring discredit on her husband, nor therefore on herself.

24   In a secondary study published in 1977, *John Stuart Mill in Love*, Josephine Kamm writes (p. 41):

> As to the supposition that Mill was impotent, the nervous complaints which afflicted him makes this sound more than possible, but there is no direct evidence either way ... Harriet, then, was unattainable, though whether as a consequence of Mill's incompetence or because he imposed an iron discipline on his natural urges we do not know.

25 A number of secondary sources describe Mill as the 'father of Victorian Liberalism'.

Now write two or three paragraphs (a couple of pages) on 'The Life of John Stuart Mill'.

 Specimen answer

Here are three different attempts which, as I hope you will see at once, are of very different levels of attainment.

Passage A

John Stuart Mill published three books showing strong Liberal sympathies: *The Principles of Political Economy* (1848), *On Liberty* (1859) and *The Subjection of Women* (1869). He also showed his independence of mind and radical principles in his election to parliament in 1865 for Westminster. In 1830, twenty-four years after his birth in London, the eldest son of the Scottish philosopher, historian and senior administrator in the East India Company's London office, James Mill, he met Mrs Harriet Taylor (then aged twenty-two), the wife of John Taylor, a prosperous London merchant. He had been educated at home by his father, starting Greek at the age of three, and learning Latin, Chemistry and the Differential Calculus before he was twelve. His independent radical views showed again when he was arrested in 1823, though not imprisoned, for distributing birth-control propaganda. Essays published between 1831 and 1840 showed his interest in both Romantic Poetry and Political Radicalism. He had a mental breakdown during the winter of 1826–7, and severe illnesses in 1836 (following the death of his father) and 1854. At the age of seventeen, in 1823, he secured his first job as clerk in his father's office, eventually in 1856 achieving the same senior post that his father had held. In 1858 the government took over the administration of the East India Company; again Mill showed his strong principles by resigning. In 1868 he lost his parliamentary seat.

In 1849 John Taylor died. Ever since 1830 Mill had been dining with Mrs Taylor two or three times a week (while her husband dined at his club), and he and Mrs Taylor travelled frequently together in England and on the Continent. Two years after Taylor's death Mill and Harriet were married. Three years later Mill started writing his autobiography, which he finally revised in 1870, and which was published in 1873. Meanwhile Harriet died in 1858, Mill himself dying in 1873. During discussions of the Reform Bill in 1867 Mill had tried to have votes extended to women, but was unsuccessful.

In 1844 when Harriet was abroad, Mill wrote to her asking for her help with the passage in his autobiography describing their relationship before they were married. This letter brings out his deep love for, and dependence upon, Harriet, and also the fact that their conduct had aroused 'scandalous suspicions'. In a passage which eventually appeared in the autobiography it was stated 'that our relation to each other at that time was of strong affection and confidential intimacy only'. The passage also makes it clear that the couple did not accept Victorian taboos on extra-marital sex, but that their behaviour was designed to avoid bringing discredit on Mr Taylor and 'therefore', as the passage puts it, on Harriet herself. However, it has been suggested that the real reason for the sexual innocence of the relationship was that Mill was impotent. Given the nervous complaints which afflicted him, this, Josephine Kamm has suggested, is more than possible, but in the nature of the evidence we simply do not know.

Passage B

John Stuart Mill was born in London in 1806, the eldest son of the Scottish philosopher, historian and senior administrator in the East India Company's London office, James Mill. Between 1809 and 1820 he was educated at home by his father, starting Greek at the age of three, and learning Latin, Chemistry and the Differential Calculus before he was twelve. In 1823 he secured his first job as a clerk in the East India Company's London office; and in the same year he was arrested, but not imprisoned, for distributing birth-control propaganda. In 1830 he met Mrs Harriet Taylor (then aged twenty-two), the wife of John Taylor, a prosperous London merchant. Clearly he fell in love with her, and between 1830 and 1849 he dined with her two or three times a week tête-à-tête while her husband dined at his club, and he travelled frequently with her in England and on the Continent. According to the autobiography their 'relation to each other at that time was of strong affection and confidential intimacy only'. Between 1831 and 1840 he published many essays demonstrating his interest in both Romantic Poetry and Political Radicalism. In 1836 he had a severe illness following the death of his father. His *Principles of Political Economy* was published in 1848, revealing his sympathies for the working class. In 1849 John Taylor died, and two years later Mill and Harriet were married. He had another severe illness in 1854, when he began writing his autobiography. Troubled by how he should present his relationship with Harriet, who was abroad at the time, he wrote to her in loving terms enlisting her help in drafting this particular passage. While revealing that neither he nor Harriet considered 'the ordinances of society binding on a subject so entirely personal', he explained that he wished to bring no discredit on Taylor nor, therefore, on Harriet. However, there has been speculation that the real reason for this sexual abstinence was Mill's impotence: it is impossible to settle the matter one way or the other. Meanwhile Mill had been rising in the East India Company, and in 1856 achieved the senior post which had once been held by his father. In 1858 Harriet died, and in the same year the government took over the administration of the East India Company: being opposed to government control of private enterprise, Mill resigned his post. The following year *On Liberty*, the classic exposition of Liberal principles, was published. Having stipulated that he would neither spend money nor canvass for votes, and that he must be free from considering only the purely local interests of his constituents, Mill agreed to stand for parliament and was elected as Radical Liberal MP for Westminster in 1865. During the debates on the 1867 Reform Bill, he tried unsuccessfully to have the vote extended to women. In the general election of the following year he lost his seat.

Mill's advocacy of political equality for women continued with the publication in 1869 of *The Subjection of Women*. The following year he completed the final revision of his autobiography, which was published three years later in the same year as his own death.

Passage C

Born in London in 1806, the eldest son of the Scottish philosopher, historian and senior administrator in the East India Company's London office, James Mill, John Stuart Mill was educated at home by his father, and became a clerk in his father's office in 1823. He rose steadily and eventually in 1858 he reached the same senior post that once had been held by his father. However, when the government two years later took over the administration of the East India Company, Mill, who was opposed to government control of private enterprise, resigned; evidently he had sufficient income from other sources. His strong principles were demonstrated again when, on being invited to stand as Radical Liberal candidate for Westminster, he agreed only on the conditions that he would neither spend money nor canvass for votes, and that he must be free to consider wider issues than the purely local ones directly affecting his constituents.

Mill is widely recognized as the father of Victorian liberalism. He had shown his radical sentiments as early as 1823 when he was arrested, though not imprisoned, for distributing birth-control propaganda. Many of his essays published between 1831 and 1840 showed him to be the voice of radicalism. During the parliamentary debates on the 1867 Reform Bill he tried unsuccessfully to have the franchise extended to women. His three major political works, *Principles of Political Economy*, in which he showed his sympathy for the working class, *On Liberty*, a classical statement of Victorian liberalism, and *The Subjection of Women*, which advocated political equality for women, were published respectively in 1848, 1859 and 1869.

Mill was evidently something of a prodigy, learning Greek at the age of three, and mastering many other difficult subjects before he was twelve. But his great intellectual achievements were not realized without cost: he had a mental breakdown during the winter of 1826–7, and severe illnesses in 1836 and 1854, the first following the death of his father (who was clearly a profound influence on him). The other great influence seems to have been Harriet Taylor, whom Mill met in 1830 when she was the wife of John Taylor, a prosperous London merchant. Mill's relationship with Harriett Taylor, in whose company he was constantly to be found during her husband's lifetime, has been the subject of much speculation at the time, and since. In his autobiography, in the writing of which he enlisted the help of Harriet, Mill declared that the relationship was 'of strong affection and confidential intimacy only'. Given his strong demonstration of principle on other issues, there seems little reason to doubt his principles on this matter, even if they read slightly curiously today: he claimed that his first concern was to avoid bringing discredit upon Mr Taylor and thus, through her husband, upon Harriet herself. Possibly a third influence on Mill was that of the Romantic poets. His parliamentary career lasted only three years but at least he had shown himself a participant in the practical world of politics as well as a political philosopher. He died in 1873, leaving the autobiography and also his letters to Harriet as valuable sources for his private life.

Discussion

I am sure you can see that *C* is better as communication then either *A* or *B*. In *A*, the pieces of information have simply been incorporated in their original order without any attempt to organize the material in any intelligent way. In *B*, the material has been brought together in chronological order. This is better, but not completely satisfactory. In *C*, a definite plan has been followed, starting with the basic facts of Mill's life, then going on to his achievements, then saying some things about his private life which might throw light on these achievements. In *C* there is a much greater attempt at *interpretation*, reading between the lines, as it were, to suggest the influence of his father and of his wife (and note the way the information about the Romantic poets was split off from the information about his early radicalism, and given rather a different use and weighting). Also *C* has been much more selective, not quoting at length but getting the essence out of the long quotations from the letter and the autobiography. You may well have found the personal information fascinating, but in writing history you have to ask yourself how significant it is compared with the achievements of Mill which really are of historical importance.

On Mill's personal life, let us refer back briefly to the previous section: again we have an example of the imperfect and fragmentary nature of historical sources which will never let us know for certain the true facts of Mill's relationship with Harriet Taylor. However, the point I am making here is that while history must above all be firmly grounded in the sources, the person who does not present the material in good organized English has failed to complete the tasks of an historian. Your answer will probably have differed quite considerably from all three of the ones given here. There is never an absolutely correct way of doing things in history or the arts. But now check through your answer to see if it is as well organized and well presented as it might be. It is always worth remembering that if your presentation is bad, the reader may not be able to follow your facts, however laboriously discovered, or your ideas, however brilliant.

7 THE BASIC ELEMENTS OF FORM AND STRUCTURE IN HISTORICAL WRITING

Passages *A* and *B* in the last exercise in section 6 do not communicate a very clear statement about John Stuart Mill because they are badly organized, that is to say they lack *form*. *A* is particularly weak because it simply sets down the pieces of information about John Stuart Mill in the order in which they have been noted down from the various sources, without any attempt to place them in logical sequence. *B* is rather better because it has at least arranged the information in chronological sequence: that is, beginning with his birth and working through his life. The trouble here is that each fact – important and unimportant – is given equal weight; and there is no attempt to establish any meaningful relationship between the different facts.

Of course, form or organization is required in any piece of writing, not just historical writing. The point is that facts and ideas thrown together in any kind of haphazard sequence simply will not communicate themselves to someone else; indeed, disorderly presentation usually suggests that the writer himself or herself is not completely clear in his or her own mind. To grasp something quickly and firmly, the human mind demands orderliness: it is fairly easy to grasp the contents of a bookshelf in which the books are arranged systematically by subject; it is much less easy to do so when the books are crammed in anyhow, or even when (as has been known) they are arranged in accordance with the colour of their binding.

In writing, the basic purpose of organization is to get the emphasis right, to direct the reader away from less important matter, while making sure that he or she has grasped the really important information.

 Exercise

Read the following passage.

1 Say in a few lines what is wrong with it.

2 Rewrite it so that it communicates more clearly.

> Nicholas, Tsar of Russia, saw himself as the defender of the Greek Orthodox Church. In recent years Greek Orthodox monks had looked after the 'Holy Places'. These were churches and shrines in the Turkish province of Palestine associated with the life of Christ. In France Napoleon III was trying to restore the popularity of his regime. Roman Catholics wanted to regain the share in the 'Holy Places' they had once had, and they had the support of Napoleon. British governments feared Russian designs on Turkey and on India and British public opinion disliked the autocratic Tsarist regime. When the Crimean War broke out certain pacifists, like Cobden and Bright, opposed it and it was the first war covered by newspaper correspondents. They could now send their dispatches by telegraph. To begin with, though, the war was highly popular in Britain. Russia first claimed the right to protect all Greek Orthodox subjects in the Turkish Empire, then sent in troops. Turkey declared war in October 1853 and Russia wiped out a Turkish naval force in the Black Sea in November 1853. British and French fleets were sent to the Black Sea in January 1854. War was declared in March. This had been a story of diplomatic muddle. The war was a story of military muddle. Many subsequent commentators were to agree with Cobden and Bright that the war was futile and achieved nothing. There was great revulsion in Britain over the grim conditions in which troops suffered and died. The prime minister, Lord Aberdeen, resigned. Russian ambitions had been checked and Turkish independence was guaranteed by the Treaty of Paris, 1856. Many questions were asked about the efficiency of British government and its military organization.

 Specimen answer

1 What is wrong with this passage is that it is very disorganized. Facts and ideas tumble out in a very disorderly way. Thus, although there is obviously a good deal

of valuable information contained in the passage, it is very difficult to get from it a clear idea of the causes, course and consequences of the Crimean War.

Clearly the author has done what you may often be tempted to do in writing an essay: he has simply served up his notes as they stand, without any attempt to organize them (that is to say, to give them form and structure) in a manner that will communicate readily with someone else. There's no point in the author (or you, or anyone) saying that his facts are right, his ideas illuminating, if it is very difficult for anyone else to discover what his facts and ideas are.

2   The passage rewritten:

> The immediate cause of the Crimean War was a dispute over the 'Holy Places' – churches and shrines in the Turkish province of Palestine associated with the life of Christ – between Greek Orthodox monks, who had established control of them in recent years, and Roman Catholics who wished to reassert their former position. Anxious to restore his popularity in France, Napoleon III championed the Catholics, while Tsar Nicholas of Russia saw himself as the defender of the Greek Orthodox Church. Behind this relatively trivial dispute lay a deep antagonism between Britain and Russia: British governments feared Russian designs on Turkey and on India and British public opinion disliked the autocratic Tsarist regime. War, formally declared by Turkey in October 1853, broke out between Russia and Turkey after the former first claimed the right to protect all Greek Orthodox subjects in the Turkish Empire, then sent in troops. After Russia had wiped out a Turkish fleet in the Black Sea, British and French fleets were sent in (January 1854). In March this story of diplomatic muddle culminated in a British and French declaration of war on Russia. Although certain pacifists, such as Cobden and Bright, opposed it, the war was highly popular. However, the grim facts of military muddle soon brought revulsion; this was the first war to be covered by military correspondents, who could now send their dispatches by telegraph. The prime minister, Lord Aberdeen, resigned, and a domestic consequence of the war was that many questions were now asked about the efficiency of British government and its military organization. The main international consequence was that Russian ambitions had been checked, while Turkish independence was guaranteed by the Treaty of Paris, 1856. Thus for all the muddle and unnecessary suffering, it was not completely true that the war achieved nothing as many subsequent commentators maintained.

Discussion

Rewriting the passage is not nearly as easy as saying what is wrong with it. Nonetheless the firmer grasp we establish now of the basic principles set out here, the better equipped you will be in the future both to write and read history and, indeed, to write on other subjects as well.

The secret (as with all writing, including your own essay writing) is:

1   Break the material down into separate single ideas (for example, the opposition of pacifists like Cobden and Bright has to be separated from the fact that this was the first war covered by newspaper correspondents).

2   Distinguish between main points and supporting points (although the point about newspaper correspondents and telegraphs is fascinating in itself, it is secondary and supplementary to the main account being given of the Crimean War – of course, it would be totally different if the main content of the passage was concerned with newspapers and technological advance).

3   Establish the links between ideas (for example, between Napoleon III's desire for popularity and his support for Catholic claims in Palestine; or between the British public's dislike of the autocratic Tsarist regime, and the popularity of the war when it broke out).

4   Above all, have a systematic plan, and make it clear what that plan is. In the revised passage, we work logically from:

(a)   the *immediate* cause of the war – the dispute over the Holy places;

(b)   the *background* cause of the war – the rivalry and hostility between Britain and Russia;

(c)   the precise events leading to the outbreak of war, and British involvement in it;

(d)   the different, and changing, reactions to the war in Britain;

(e)   the consequences of the war – domestic, and then international;

(f)   general summing up.

5   Avoid unexplained contradictions, as between the view that the war achieved nothing, and the view that it resulted in the checking of Russian ambitions and the raising of questions about British government and military organization. In the rewritten version the former view is mentioned, but the conclusion, on balance, rejects it.

I don't suppose your revised version was identical to mine. You may have adopted a different plan, and have come up with something equally good. The vital point is to get things sorted out and to be absolutely clear what it is you are trying to say. Then say it in the simplest possible way. By all means exploit the infinite richness of the English language, but if you do choose elaborate words and phrases, make sure they are the right ones, that they say exactly what you mean. Do not use such words and phrases merely in an attempt to show off; they are more likely to show you up.

 # 8 SELECTION IN HISTORICAL WRITING

Problems of form and organization are common to any type of writing. Another problem common to all writing, but particularly acute in historical writing, is the problem of *selection*. The human past is so rich and complex, and so enormous, that no historian, even if dealing with a relatively short period in time, could set down everything that happened in that time. Nor would he or she wish to do so. The historian is concerned with those events, and interconnections between events, that are *significant*. The good historian knows which facts to select and which to reject when he or she is producing a piece of written history. It is again impossible to lay down absolute rules. Depending on the kind of history they are writing, different historians will single out different pieces of information as significant. As we saw in the passage about the Crimean War, it would have been better if the original author had selected for himself one definite opinion about whether the Crimean War achieved anything or not.

Any historian writing a scholarly book will need to consult a vast range of primary and secondary sources but again, of course, he will have to *select* only a small number of passages which are directly relevant to his book. As a famous Cambridge historian of Victorian England (and the tutor who, as Best tells us, first awakened his interest in Victorian Britain), Dr Kitson Clark has said: 'One of the earliest and most painful lessons which a young researcher must master is that much that he has discovered with difficulty, and with some exaltation, will prove in due course to be of no significance and of no imaginable interest, and in the end will have to be left out' (*Guide for Research Students Working in Historical Subjects*, p. 31).

In writing your own essays as a student you will encounter this very same problem of selection. However hard you have worked, and however much material you have collected, in the end you must be sure to include in your essay only what is relevant to the subject you are writing about. Often more important than what you put in is what you leave out.

 Exercise

Imagine you are taking notes for an essay on 'How far did the living conditions of the urban poor in Victorian Britain vary from place to place; in general were they improving or getting worse?' and you are using as your source (for a proper essay, of course, you would use several sources) the section of chapter 1 of Best entitled 'Public Health and Civic Amenities', pages 73–84. Try to arrive at a list of main headings, rather than a long list of lots of detailed and perhaps overlapping points. Above all avoid listing headings or points that do not definitely relate to the particular question asked.

 Specimen answer

Differences from place to place

1   Infant mortality rates very bad in Liverpool, not quite so bad in Manchester, better still in Glasgow.

2   The rent is much higher in London than in the Midlands and the North.

3   Overcrowding much worse in Yorkshire than in Lancashire, even worse in the North East, and worse still in Scotland; however, single rooms in Scotland were larger and better equipped.

4   Grime common to all towns.

5   Despite variations already noted, overcrowding and proximity to work were common factors.

Getting worse

1   Diphtheria

2   Overcrowded central districts got worse because of commercial redevelopments, railway works, and so on. Also cheap housing almost always lagged behind demand.

Getting better

1   Decline in 'filth' diseases.

2   Decline in death rate of older children.

3   New civic amenities, such as parks.

 Discussion

It would be useful to quote from the statistics in the table on page 74, but you should point out that strictly speaking these, and the general comments on the first few pages, refer to the population as a whole; however, since the urban poor were so numerous, the statistics can be taken as a reasonably accurate representation of their condition. In writing an essay you would have to give an answer to the question 'how far?': from the information derived from Best, something along the lines of 'while there were considerable regional variations in detail, the general condition of the urban poor across the country was fairly miserable' would be reasonable. You would also have to give an answer to the question of whether matters were getting better or worse, and here Best's opening point is highly relevant: that the achievement in public health 'was the great one, considering all the circumstances, of preventing the cities from becoming even more lethal than they already were'. An appropriate answer to this question would be that overall living conditions were improving slightly, particularly after 1875, but that there were setbacks in certain areas, particularly that of overcrowding.

In writing an essay, of course, not only do you have to collect the relevant information (and rigorously exclude everything that is irrelevant), you have to be sure that you give clear answers to the questions asked.

I was being selective when, in Unit 1, I suggested that the best way to study the aspects of Victorian society of most relevance to this course would be to settle for six headings.

 Exercise

Can you remember what those headings were?

 Specimen answer

1   Basic features of the economy
2   Social conditions
3   Town and country
4   Industrialization and the social structure
5   Culture and belief
6   The major changes in Victorian society from the 1870s onwards

9   NARRATIVE, ANALYSIS AND DESCRIPTION

Historical writing can be broken down into three categories: narrative, analysis and description.

Narrative is essential for conveying the sense of change through time which lies at the core of all historical writing (Unit 1, section 4). Narrative takes us through from an earlier point in time to a later one.

In the case of, say, a political history of Britain 1850–68, a narrative account will start by noting that in 1850 a Whig government was in office under the prime ministership of Lord John Russell and then proceed to a chronological account of the succeeding changes in government: Lord Derby and the Tories took over in February 1852, lasting only until December 1852 when a government of Whigs and Peelite Tories was formed under Lord Aberdeen; its mismanagement of the Crimean War brought this ministry down in January 1855 and a Whig government under Lord Palmerston took over; Palmerston had to give way to Lord Derby in January 1859, returning triumphantly to office in June, where he remained until his death in October 1865; Russell now became prime minister, but resigned in June 1866 during discussions of his proposed second reform bill. Derby and the Conservatives took over, and were responsible for passing the Reform Act of 1867, Disraeli succeeding Derby in February 1868; the general elections of 1868 gave a clear majority to Gladstone (and the Liberals, as they now called themselves).

This kind of historical writing may have a familiar ring; perhaps you have encountered it in school textbooks. It is fine, and necessary, as far as it goes, and for some kinds of political and military history narrative may well provide the main drive. The trouble is that although we get the sequence of events, we do not get any kind of description or explanation of them.

A narrative account of mid-Victorian politics does not tell us *why* so many prime ministers succeeded each other with such rapidity, does not tell us what it meant to be a Whig or a Tory, nor explain how Whigs became Liberals and Tories became Conservatives; we are left in puzzlement as to how in the end it was the Conservatives who passed the Second Reform Act, and we learn nothing about the significance of this act.

It is the function of *analysis* to deal with these vital questions of explanation, relationship, meaning and achievement. *Description* is in the end perhaps less important than either narrative or analysis, but we do need it sometimes just to tell us what was actually in a particular book or document, or what conditions of life were like at a certain time.

Most often in historical writing, analysis and description will be mingled together. They share a common feature in that while narrative is concerned with change through time, both analysis and description extract some topic from the time process and look at it as if it were static: a narrative account of Victorian politics lists changes in chronological sequence; description and analysis would look at a series of topics in turn – for example, 'The Rule of the Aristocracy', 'The Political Parties', 'The Electorate', 'Whigs and Tories, Liberals and Conservatives', 'The Franchise and Parliamentary Reform'.

Although description and analysis involve the same method of presentation – presentation by topic – and although they are usually mingled together, we can make a clear distinction between them. Analysis performs the more rigorous, intellectual task. Description will tell us what sort of politics Whigs and Tories stood for, the provisions of the Reform Act; analysis will reveal the nature of the mid-Victorian political system, how it differed from politics today, why all prime ministers from 1850 to February 1868 were aristocrats, and so on.

In historical writing, if you, or the historian, are to achieve a sense of movement through time, it is always necessary to counterbalance description and analysis on the one side with sufficient narrative on the other side. But in *all* types of writing, including history, if you are to achieve sufficient intellectual rigour, you must counterbalance any narrative and description (the easier aspects) with sufficient analysis.

Sometimes historical works, particularly if they deal with a relatively short space of time, consist almost exclusively of analysis and description, without any narration.

 Exercise

You should be familiar with one such work. Say what it is and add a sentence explaining your answer.

 Specimen answer and discussion

Best's *Mid-Victorian Britain 1851–75*. This covers a fairly short period of time and is essentially broken up by topics, for example, 'The Urban Environment', 'The Cult of Work', describing and analysing mid-Victorian Britain with no chronological account of events. In part this is because Best is writing social, not political history, though it is possible to have narrative in social history (a chronology of Public Health Acts, for example).

 Exercise

In Best, read the following three passages. Indicate whether each is *predominantly* description (*D*) or analysis (*A*).

(a)   The passage on pages 68–9 entitled 'Edinburgh'. ☐

(b)   The paragraph starting near the top of page 75 and running almost half-way down page 76. ☐

(c)   The first paragraph of 'Children at Work', pages 129–32. ☐

(d)   The paragraph that begins towards the foot of page 196 and runs to the middle of page 197. ☐

Specimen answers and discussion

(a) *D*   (b) *A*   (c) *A*   (d) *D*

I hope you can see that (a) is basically Best telling us what Edinburgh *was like*, that is describing it, rather than raising and answering big questions; and that similarly in (d) he is simply reporting the findings of investigations which *describe* the religious structures in England. However, (b) clearly raises, and in some places answers, questions (London was safer than Berlin): it is analysing. I will admit that (c) has quite a strong descriptive element, and I can sympathize if you were misled here – but if you look closely you'll see that Best is analysing conditions to find out how bad they were.

If you still cannot get the right answers, please go back and re-read the whole of this section so far.

 Exercise

Turn to F. M. L. Thompson's 'The Decline of the Landed Interest' in the Supplementary Material booklet, and read the first three paragraphs. In a sentence, discuss whether the paragraphs are predominantly narrative, analysis or description.

 Specimen answer

While they are far from being a simple narrative account, and contain much analysis (for example, that aristocrats were responsible for the demolition of aristocratic institutions, with possible reasons) and description (for example, of the arguments put to the Marquess of Bath), essentially these paragraphs do convey a narrative of events affecting the aristocracy from the first Reform Bill (1832) through to the third (1886).

You may have had difficulties with this one, but I hope that on reflection you will see that these paragraphs carry the main narrative function of the chapter, taking us through from 1832 to 1886; while the rest of the chapter, in fact, is almost exclusively analysis and description.

The differences between narrative, analysis and description will often stand out more clearly in an entire book, rather than in one short chapter or article. Usually, though there are many exceptions, such as Best's book, a historian will try to achieve a balance between narrative, analysis and description.

There are five basic methods of achieving such a balance:

1   Divide the material up by topic, but *within each topic observe a narrative sequence.*

2   Alternate passages of narrative with passages of description and analysis.

3   Divide the material up by time sequence into a number of sub-periods, thus giving a broad sense of narrative flow. Then within each sub-period deal with the material topic by topic.

4   A mixture of these: for example, some chapters that are entirely by topic (description and analysis) for the entire period covered by the book, and some chapters that cover sub-periods.

5   'Narrative thickened by analysis' (the phrase is that of Professor G. R. Elton). In general follow a traditional narrative pattern, but whenever a logical need arises for description and analysis, stop the narrative and provide the necessary descriptive and analytical material. The three paragraphs by Thompson we just looked at were, in fact, 'narrative thickened by analysis'.

 Exercise

Here is the table of contents for the entire book, *English Landed Society in the Nineteenth Century* (the chapter 'The Decline of the Landed Interest' is reproduced in the Supplementary Material booklet). Judging from this table of contents, which of the methods (1–5) given above does Thompson follow in achieving a balance between narrative, analysis and description? (The overall emphasis it may be noted is, as with most serious academic studies, on analysis.)

I	The Nature of Landed Society
II	Aristocratic England
III	The Institution of the Landed Aristocracy
IV	The Life of a Landed Aristocrat
V	The Landed Gentry and County Society
VI	The Management of the Landed Estates
VII	Landowners and the Local Community
VIII	Landed Estates in War and Peace, 1770–1835
IX	Estates in the Railway Age, 1835–80
X	The Decline of the Landed Interest, 1830–80
XI	Indian Summer, 1880–1914
XII	Eclipse, 1914–39

 Specimen answer

Chapters I to VII are defined purely by topic, but from VIII onwards sub-periods are introduced, in X and XII purely for the purpose of giving us a sense of *narrative* of the declining fortunes of the Landed Interest as a whole.

 Discussion

I would not be surprised if you are not completely happy about all this. One can really only clearly perceive the distinctions between narrative, analysis and description when one has lots of examples to compare. Still, try to get the basic distinctions in mind now, appreciating that a complete historical work will usually be a balance of all three: narrative *tells a story*, analysis and description cut across the story, looking at the past *topic by topic*. As you read more historical books for yourself, try to work out the structure of narrative, analysis and description on which the book is based.

10 PLANNING A HISTORY ESSAY

You have to know how to select relevant material. But once you have selected your material, as I have already stressed, you have to communicate it. Writing a student history essay, obviously, is not as complicated as writing an entire history book, though in essence the problems are similar. Let us, however, concentrate on the sort of essay you are likely to be asked to write during your student career.

Usually any essay subject which you are set will take the form of asking you a direct question, though it may be in the form, say, of presenting you with a definite statement or point of view, which you are then asked to discuss. The first obvious point is: whatever the exact form of the question, always be sure to answer the question asked, not some other question you would like to have been asked, or some other question which relates to the one asked but is not exactly the one asked. You will be expected to give a balanced answer, weighing up the pros and cons, but ultimately making it quite clear to your reader what answer you are giving. If you are asked a direct question you must give a definite answer, however much you may feel it necessary to express qualifications, to explain the complexities. If the question is in the form of asking you to discuss some proposition, you must make it clear whether you are agreeing or disagreeing with the proposition. Like any historian, you will be presenting your interpretation. To do this, you will need to *analyse* your material, not simply unload information or present a straight narrative. In writing essays students are often tempted to narrate for nine-tenths of the space at their disposal, then try to make up for this with a solid lump of analysis at the end. This is a lazy and unsatisfactory way of writing an essay. When you are writing an essay, you should show that you are *thinking all the time*, not simply setting down information. Try to be sure that *every* sentence, *every* phrase even, is making a positive contribution to the interpretation which you are developing and is not simply set down because you think it might have some bearing on the question asked, though you are not quite clear in your own mind exactly what. As already indicated, you must be selective in the material you include, making sure that it is relevant to the question you have been asked. Finally, you must organize your material, both within individual paragraphs, and in the essay as a whole, so that the answer you are giving communicates as effectively as possible with the reader. To achieve a properly organized essay, it is highly desirable to set out a plan for it in advance.

Imagine you're faced with the following essay subject:

'Mid-Victorian Britain was still essentially a society of orders and estates; only in the 1880s did it become a class society.' Discuss.

Now, to be able to answer that question properly you would have to have read the relevant parts of Best, principally chapter 4, but also parts of chapter 3, and some elements from chapter 2, F. M. L. Thompson's chapter on 'The Decline of the Landed Interest', François Bédarida's chapter on 'The Crisis of Victorian Values' (both reproduced in the Supplementary Material booklet), and the relevant primary documents. You should not start planning an essay until you have done a good deal of reading and, as it were, got the 'feel' of the subject. However, on the basis of the discussion we have already had on the topic of class, let us see what sort of plan we might come up with. It would be wise to make it clear what you understand by mid-Victorian Britain, the period which you are asked to contrast with the 1880s. Presumably, you would take mid-Victorian Britain to be the period covered by Best, that is to say 1851–75. Then you would have to take the first part of the question, working out the pros and cons of the statement that 'mid-Victorian Britain was essentially a society of estates and orders'. This would in part contribute to answering the second part of the question that 'only in the 1880s did Britain become a class society', but you would now have to look at the 1880s to see in what ways, if any, the social structure was different from what it had been in the earlier period. So there, for a start, we have a broad division of the essay into two parts.

But you'll need some kind of structure for each part. You might just decide on the very simple structure of the first stating the arguments in favour of the part of the statement being discussed, then arguments against (or *vice versa*), but it would be possible, and desirable, to work out a more detailed structure than that. You know that by a 'class society' we mean a society that has two or more classes – say, an upper class, a middle class, and a working class, to take the simplest formula. You could then structure each half of the essay by looking at each of these broad categories in turn asking, in the first part of the essay, what evidence suggests that there is indeed an upper class (and then in turn, a middle class, and a working class) and, therefore, signs of a class society, and what evidence suggests that, on the contrary, instead of classes such as these we still have estates and orders.

A plan for an essay along these lines might look something like this:

Part I   Mid-Victorian Britain 1850–1875

1   'Upper class'

(a)   Arguments for the existence of a definite class
You might, following Best and Thompson, argue that the dominant class was still the landed aristocracy or you might argue that, despite appearances, real power already lay with an industrial middle class.

(b)   Arguments against
You would have to note the arguments from Best that between the landed aristocracy and other social groups there were vertical links, rather than the horizontal divides of class. You might also make the point that the continued dominance of a landed aristocracy smacked more of a pre-industrial society of orders and estates rather than of an industrial class society. Even if you preferred to stress the significance of the industrial bourgeoisie, you would have to take account of the points made by Best and Thompson.

(c)   Conclusions to this section

(i)   You could conclude that the clear dominance of the landed aristocracy did mean the existence at this level of strong elements of a class society, even if it was a different kind of class society from what came later, or

(ii)   you could argue that because dominance still lay with the landed aristocracy as it had done in an older society of estates and orders, one cannot really discern real elements of class at this level, or

(iii)   you could argue that despite the continuing prestige and status of the landed aristocracy, strong elements of an industrial class society were already in being.

2   'Middle classes'

(a)   Arguments in favour of there being a distinctive class at this level
Using Best you could point to the evidence of there being a social group (of industrialists, bankers, professional people, and so on) deferential towards the aristocracy above, and conscious of their superiority to the workers below – that is to say, a genuine *middle* class. You could also cite evidence from Thompson of some of the ways in which this class was in fact critical of, and even opposed to, the landed aristocracy. Or, of course, you might continue the argument that this class was already taking over from the landed aristocracy, in which case you might want to concentrate on 'middling' or 'transitional' groups at the bottom of the middle class. Using Best you could point to the way in which education clearly distinguished the middle class from the working class.

(b)   Arguments against
You could use Best to point to the enormous range of occupations that would have to be grouped within the term 'middle class', so enormous as to perhaps make the term 'class' meaningless. You could also again cite Best's point about vertical links, and his point about the basic distinction merely being between respectable and not respectable, rather than between distinct classes. Using Best and Thompson, you could point to the continuing importance of the countryside with its own social structure, which is rather different from that of an industrial class structure.

(c)   Conclusion
You could well conclude that the very range and variety of middle or middling occupations, the persistence of traditional occupations, and the links between small businessmen and artisans and craftsmen, make it unrealistic to talk of a middle class in mid-Victorian Britain. Or, taking the line that class is never a simple subject, but always has its complexities and exceptions, you could come to the opposite conclusion, though you would have to give due weight to the complexities and exceptions.

3   'Working class'

(a)   Arguments for the existence of a definite working class
You could point to the existence of trade unions and definite examples of workers organizing to defend and advance their own interests. You could point to Horace Mann's clear recognition of the existence of a working class with particular attitudes and problems of its own. You could use Best's discussion of wages to show that there definitely was a large class of people very different in living standards and living conditions from people above them in society.

(b)   Arguments against
You could point out that trade unions were mainly confined to the more skilled and better-off workers. You could again point to the immense range and variety of occupations, and to the persistence of traditional occupations, particularly in rural areas. Indeed, you could argue that with over 40 per cent of the population still in rural areas one cannot yet speak of the existence of a national working class. You could again refer to Best's points about vertical links and the basic division between respectable and unrespectable. You could argue that rather than a working class, what mid-Victorian society had was a vast amorphous mass, the poor and under-employed, just as had existed in the older society of estates and orders.

(c)   Conclusion
This could range from arguing that a working class had already come into existence, to that it was coming into existence but that for many parts of the country the phrase 'lower orders' would be more appropriate, to the argument that no real working class yet existed.

4   Relationships between social groups

(a)   Arguments for
How much weight you put on this will depend upon how far you go with E. P. Thompson in seeing class as a relationship and how far, on the contrary, you see class as a means of mapping society. But whichever broad view you take, there are important points to debate here. On the pro-class side is the evidence of violence and hostility between employers and employees, the contempt and snobbishness shown by aristocrats for the middle class, and by the middle class for the working class – though interpreted differently this could be used to demonstrate the existence of traditional estates and orders rather than classes; the organization of parliament to express aristocratic interests, though with growing middle-class pressure, the voicing of middle-class interests in the cities.

(b)   Arguments against
The evidence of general social harmony and moderate reform; the points stressed by Best.

5   Overall conclusion to Part I
One would expect this to be some version of the view that in mid-Victorian Britain elements of class existed side-by-side with the older elements of estates and orders, which way you tipped the balance depending upon how you interpreted the evidence. If you put great weight on the elements of class this would lead you on to casting doubt on the validity of the second part of the statement under discussion.

Part II   The 1880s

As we have noted there are really two parts to the second phrase: did a class society appear in the 1880s, and did it *only* appear in the 1880s? We can again apply these two questions in turn to our three broad categories.

1   'Upper class'

(a)   Bédarida suggests that there are two 'governing classes', the 'aristocracy' and the 'bourgeoisie', Thompson that the aristocratic class is giving way to the industrial class and, to some degree, amalgamating with it; in extract I.19 in the

Course Reader, T. H. S. Escott gives a clear impression of one upper class composed of aristocratic, commercial, industrial and professional elements. If we lay emphasis on the two separate upper classes, rather than one amalgamated upper class, we could argue that a true upper class has not yet appeared. If we lay stress on the amalgamation then we could argue that a new kind of upper class has appeared, different from anything that existed in the mid-Victorian period.

(b)   Whether we say that it *only* appeared in the 1880s depends on how we argued in Part I.

2   'Middle class'

(a)   Your reading would not be a lot of help here, but you may remember my suggestion that a genuine middle class now emerged which could in no way be conceived of as being part of the upper class; against that it could be argued that all the old complexities still existed and so again one could argue that a definite middle class had not yet appeared.

(b)   My suggestion would be that only now with the blending of the most successful industrial elements into the upper class do we have a clarity in the class structure, but against that it could be argued that the same sort of genuinely middle group was already apparent in mid-Victorian Britain.

3   'Working class'

(a)   There is now unionization among the unskilled workers so that we have a larger and more integrated working class; rural elements are clearly in decline, yet still there are divisions within the working class and the existence of the residuum.

(b)   Definitely there is a bigger, better organized, and more aggressive working class than there was in the mid-Victorian period, yet it would be hard to deny that some sort of working class definitely did exist in the mid-Victorian period.

4   Relationships

(a)   Bédarida brings out very well the sharpening of antagonism between classes, though he also stresses the growth of middle-class, as he sees it, sympathy for the plight of the working class. Notions of different classes and their different conditions do seem to be more explicit. Thompson brings out the growing assertiveness of the industrial class.

Part III   Overall conclusion

This would have to be some form of argument that the statement for discussion contains an important truth in that social structure in the 1880s was different from what it had been in the mid-Victorian period, but that the statement needs qualification for either or both of the following reasons:

1   there were strong elements of class already apparent in mid-Victorian Britain;

2   a complete class structure had not in fact fully appeared in the 1880s.

I hope you can see how an essay plan is not just an arbitrary, or contrived series of headings, but is directly related to the questions that you have to raise in order to be able to deal with the question posed, and in fact is really a plan of the stages or steps in an argument.

This is not the only plan that could have been followed. An alternative, though on the whole I think a less satisfactory one, since I doubt if the arguments would emerge as clearly, would have been to make the basic division not into two periods, but into the main categories of social group, as follows:

1   'Upper class' – whether an estate or a class in the mid-Victorian period: what changed in the 1880s? Was the crucial change in the 1880s? Was there still not fully a class in the 1880s?

2   'Middle class' – a class, or a series of orders and estates in the mid-Victorian period: what changed in the 1880s? Was the crucial change in the 1880s? Was there still not fully a class in the 1880s?

3   'Working class'. Had this come into existence or not in the mid-Victorian period? Did it only come into existence, or did it come into existence fully, in the 1880s?

4   Relationships. What real evidence of class feeling in the mid-Victorian period? What changes, and how crucial, in the 1880s?

5   Conclusion

Or, if you are an ambitious and confident student, you might decide to structure the whole essay on the theoretical arguments about class. This would give you a basic structure something like this:

Part I   Aristocracy, bourgeoisie and proletariat in mid-Victorian Britain

Part II   Aristocracy, bourgeoisie and proletariat in the 1880s

But you still would be wise to work out detailed sub-headings within that broad pattern.

 Exercise

Imagine you have to write an essay on the following:

> 'Mid-Victorian Britain was a prudish, hypocritical society without real political or cultural achievement; the real achievements came in the period 1875–1880.' Do you agree?

Now I want you to try to draw up a plan for this essay. Even if you feel, quite understandably, that you have insufficient information to be able to make points and to suggest possible alternative conclusions in the way I did in my plan, try at least to devise a structure of brief headings indicating the issues you would have to raise and the order in which you would raise them. I would like you to make a genuine attempt at this exercise; however, if you really feel that I am asking the impossible, read on, but then make a real effort to understand how I have arrived at my plan.

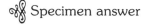 Specimen answer

(If you have got anything like my main headings you have done very well; I wouldn't really expect you also to have the sort of points I have put in brackets.)

Part I   Mid-Victorian Britain

1   Question of prudishness

(a)   Evidence of being prudish
(Gossip about John Stuart Mill; Mill's own attitudes; evidence from *Hard Times*; attitudes towards women; attitudes towards sex; attitudes towards divorce, and so on.)

(b)   Evidence and arguments against regarding Victorians as prudish
(John Stuart Mill's statement about personal morality; the argument that what we might regard as prudishness must be seen in the context of Victorian concepts of respectability.)

(c)   Conclusion
(Perhaps something along the lines that by our own standards the mid-Victorians certainly *seem* prudish but raising the question of whether in this respect the mid-Victorians were any different from those living in the period 1875–1890.)

2   Hypocrisy

(a)   Evidence of hypocrisy
(Best's remarks on Victorian religion; grinding the faces of the poor; the types represented by Mr Bounderby; resort to prostitution, and so on.)

(b)   Evidence and arguments against regarding Victorians as hypocrites
(Some genuine work for reform; forthright liberal philosophy of John Stuart Mill;

passionate commitment to religion; genuine investigation of Crimean War muddles; honourable resignation of Lord Aberdeen.)

(c)   Conclusion
(Perhaps it was their naive belief in progress which more than anything else gives the Victorians the appearance of hypocrisy in our eyes – were they really any more hypocritical than any other generation, were they more hypocritical than the generation of 1875–1890?)

3   Political achievements

(a)   (There were some achievements: for example, the Reform Act of 1867, public health measures discussed by Best.)

(b)   (Nevertheless, were these achievements seriously flawed? Were they outweighed by failures? Best points out the limitations of the public health measures, the Reform Act was certainly a very moderate measure, and it could be argued that the failures of the Crimean War outweigh everything else.)

4   Cultural achievements

(a)   (Well, you might think to mention *Hard Times* and perhaps other novels by Dickens; the remainder of this course will provide you with plenty of evidence to argue over: were the Pre-Raphaelites great innovative painters, or simply rather pathetic panders to Victorian middle-class taste? How about the Great Exhibition as a cultural achievement? If you include science and technology as part of culture then you would give the mid-Victorians high ratings here.)

(b)   Conclusion
(You might well argue that, literature – and sciences – apart, mid-Victorian cultural achievements were not great, and it might be argued, though probably incorrectly, that the Great Exhibition was more concerned with material, rather than with spiritual and cultural values.)

Part II   1875–1890

1   Any differences from mid-Victorian period in respect of prudishness and hypocrisy?
(Strictly speaking, the question as set does not *demand* that you deal with this issue, but a completely-rounded answer, fully assessing the criticism that mid-Victorian Britain was prudish and hypocritical, would need to look at how it compared with later Victorian Britain. From Bédarida you would get some suggestions that in regard to questions of sex, the family, and so on, there was some lessening in prudishness and perhaps also in hypocrisy.)

2   Political achievements
(You could argue that the 1884 Reform Act did far more than the 1867 one, or that, on the contrary, it was the 1867 one that led the way; but Bédarida does give you examples of more advanced social legislation. Whether all this adds up to truly great achievements, however, could be the matter of some discussion.)

3   Cultural achievements
(Again, later parts of the course will provide you with the material with which to arrive at an evaluation of this question. Some of the most eminent of Victorians died around 1873, for example John Stuart Mill; on the other hand newer figures, such as William Morris and Thomas Hardy, reached their peak. There was no scientific 'giant' to compare with Darwin, yet striking advances in, especially, physics continued.)

Part III Conclusion

(A reasonable conclusion might be that it is a little unfair to write off the mid-Victorians as prudish and hypocritical but that, perhaps, complacency was more widespread in the mid-Victorian period than it was in the later Victorian period, when there were more positive drives towards dealing with the great social issues and also some signs of cultural innovation.)

If you have found this section hard going, just for the moment grasp the main point that when you do come to write essays, it is important to plan them out in advance. Later in the course you may feel you want to come back to this section for the advice it offers on the basic thought processes that lie behind planning an essay and developing an argument in it.

REFERENCES

Bédarida, F. (1979) *A Social History of England 1851–1975,* Methuen. Chapter 4 'The Crisis of Victorian Values' is reprinted in the Supplementary Material booklet.

Clark, G. Kitson (1960) *Guide for Research Students Working in Historical Subjects*

Dickens, C. (1989) *Hard Times,* Oxford University Press.

Golby, J. (ed.) (1986) *Culture and Society in Britain 1850–1890: a source book of contemporary writings,* Oxford University Press (referred to in the text as the Course Reader).

Kamm, J. (1977) *John Stuart Mill in Love,* Gordon and Cremonesi.

Thompson, F. M. L. (1963) *English Landed Society in the Nineteenth Century,* Routledge and Kegan Paul. Chapter 10 'The Decline of the Landed Interest, 1830–80' is reprinted in the Supplementary Material booklet.

Unit 3

PROBLEMS OF WRITING HISTORY

SET READING

As you work through Unit 3 you will need to refer to
John Golby (ed.) (1986) *Culture and Society in Britain 1850–1890* (Course Reader)
Geoffrey Best (1979) *Mid-Victorian Britain 1851–75* (Set Book)
Supplementary Material booklet

BROADCASTING

Television programme 3 *An Historian at Work*

OBJECTIVES

Section 1 Quotations, footnotes and bibliographies

You should understand why such things as footnotes, bibliographies, and so on are essential to good historical writing.

Section 2 Types of historical communication

You should be able to distinguish between the different levels of historical writing (for example, PhD theses, text books, pop history) and be able to criticize works on each level on their own merits.

Section 3 Periodization

You should understand why in order to write history we have to chop up the past into 'periods', and you should be aware of the dangers of doing this.

Section 4 Historical semantics (or historical 'hot potatoes')

You should know how to use, and how not to use, some of the difficult words in history, such as feudalism, revolution, capitalism, class and culture.

Section 5 Controversy in historical writing

You should appreciate that historians do not just disagree with each other for the hell of it, and you should be able to explain the manner in which controversy among historians can further historical discovery.

Section 6 History and the other arts disciplines

You should appreciate the value of bringing history together with the other arts disciplines in addressing major problems and be able to discuss critically the relationship and the differences between those disciplines and history.

Section 7 Reminding you of the 'essential features' of Victorian society

You should appreciate fully the 'essential features' of Victorian society and should understand how certain of the documents in your Course Reader can be related to them.

Section 8 Conclusion and Guide to Further Reading

1 QUOTATIONS, FOOTNOTES AND BIBLIOGRAPHIES

Whether you are writing an essay, a thesis or a book you must have obtained your information from somewhere. Sometimes you may actually wish to use a quotation from a passage that you have found in your reading. This is most likely to be so if the passage is from a primary source. For example, if you are writing about John Stuart Mill's conception of liberalism you will very probably need to quote his own words.

Sometimes a passage from a primary or secondary source may seem so striking that you feel you must quote the original. There is another possible reason for quoting directly from a secondary source: it may be that you do not in fact agree with the passage that you are quoting. In this case you must quote the original words so that if necessary you can then go on to disagree with them.

It is important not to overdo the use of direct quotation. 'Scissor-and-paste' is the term we apply rather contemptuously to a piece of historical writing that looks as though the writer has simply cut up chunks of other people's work and pasted them together. Remember that quotations from other authors, however eminent, do not necessarily prove anything. In writing history you must be convinced of the validity of what you are saying. Do not attempt to hide behind quotations from other authors.

Especially in the early stages of your career, you will be quite dependent on others for most of your ideas: to some extent that is why you are studying in the first place. But you must avoid full-blooded *plagiarism*. This occurs when you steal a phrase from some other writer and pass it off as your own. If you wish to use someone else's phrase then you must use it as a direct quotation: that is you must either put it in quotation marks or indent it.

The number of times you will wish to use direct quotations will usually depend on the kind of history you are writing. If you are working extensively in primary sources then you may wish to have many direct quotations from these sources. But in your own case – with the sort of essay drawn mainly from secondary sources which you will be writing as a student – there will be less need for direct quotation. In general it is worth memorizing as a basic working rule the statement that *quotations may illustrate a point; they seldom prove it.*

Occasionally the professional historian working in the primary sources does find that a direct quotation from a new document which he has discovered, or from a passage in a document which other historians have ignored or misunderstood, may in fact serve to *prove* the point he is making. (Until John Stuart Mill's letters to his wife became available historians did not know of her influence in the writing of the part of the *Autobiography* that we looked at earlier – direct quotation from his letter does demonstrate the point very clearly.) More often for the historian, as for you, a direct quotation will simply *illustrate* a point rather than prove it. Proof in most cases depends on an argument rather than on one quotation. And this, incidentally, is another reason for stressing form and structure in historical writing. It is the entire presentation of the argument that convinces (or fails to convince) the reader, not isolated facts or quotations.

Apart from merely illustrating a point, direct quotations can often serve a very valuable purpose in conveying atmosphere. You have now encountered a number of extracts from Victorian documents and, apart from all their other uses, these certainly help to give you the 'feel' of the age in a way in which nothing else can. Direct quotations from letters, diaries, novels, poems or perhaps folk songs can all help to convey the atmosphere of a particular period in the past.

 Exercise

Turn to:

the last two pages of F. M. L. Thompson's chapter on the 'Decline of the Landed Interest, 1830–80' in the Supplementary Material booklet, from 'Behind all these changes...' to '...although their ascendancy was over.'

François Bédarida's chapter 'The Crisis of Victorian Values' in the Supplementary Material booklet and read from halfway through the seventh paragraph in the section titled '*Laissez-faire* challenged', beginning 'At the same time another more famous Booth...' to 'the ones who... gave up the comforts of respectability and patronage were not numerous.'

Best, pages 21–22, starting with the second paragraph on page 21, 'The wealth of Britain...', and reading to the end of the middle paragraph on page 22, '"... magnitude of economic expansion".'

Answer the following questions:

1 Each of these passages contains two or three quotations. Both Thompson and Bédarida use their quotations in a rather different way from Best. What is this?

2 In each case, it seems to me, the use of quotation is extremely effective. Write your own comments on what you think the direct quotations in each passage contribute to the passage as historical communication.

 Specimen answers

1 Both Thompson and Bédarida are quoting from primary sources, giving us an insight into how contemporaries saw specific issues. Best, on the other hand, is quoting from secondary sources, enlisting the help of other famous historians in establishing general points about the place of economic history in the study of history.

2 What I found particularly striking in the Thompson excerpt was the long quotation from the poem recited to the Percy dependants at a celebratory dinner. This seems to me to bring out in a particularly striking way the manner in which the social position of the landed interest was indeed largely intact. This contrasts very well with the more matter-of-fact earlier quotations from Evelyn Dennison and Lord Monson. These effectively make the point that on straight financial terms alone land was no longer the profitable commodity it used to be. But then, with the effective use of the last quotation the entire two pages bring out brilliantly how the ownership of land was not simply a matter of economic interest, but a matter of social position. Without these judicious and well chosen direct quotations I don't think Thompson could have put the point over so effectively.

In the excerpt from Bédarida we have quotations from a book and from a lecture, respectively. They illustrate most effectively the attitudes of certain middle-class people towards the poor. The quotation from William Booth, founder of the Salvation Army, brings out well the continuing moral and religious impulse – he was concerned that someone who was hungry and without lodging would be in no position to pay heed to what, revealingly, linking the New Testament and Samuel Smiles, he calls 'the gospel of Thrift'. The long quotation from Arnold Toynbee really is redolent of the guilty middle-class figure who feels he must make amends to the working-class poor.

In the first paragraph Best is trying to justify the importance of paying attention to economic facts, which might seem rather dull. He then wants to make the point that economic facts, though vitally important, are only a foundation for the really interesting work, social history. But he fears that if he just said this bluntly we might not pay too much attention, which is why he makes the direct quotation from Sir John Clapham, 'foundations exist to carry better things'. With his second quotation he is trying to give an explanation of the great credit booms which marked the mid-Victorian period. Here, it seems to me, Best is tacitly admitting that he himself is not an expert in such economic matters and thus prefers to quote a whole sentence from another very famous economic historian, H. J. Habakkuk. Quoting such an authority does not prove the point, but it lends it a kind of weight which it might not have if Best made the point without the use of the direct quotation.

 Discussion

I am sure you will not have put things in quite the way I have done, but I hope you can see that in all three cases we have very judicious and effective use of quotation. Note particularly that while with the song Thompson, for full effect, has permitted quite a long quotation, in general the quotations are short and generally incorporated within the body of a sentence. Do not pad out your work with quotations; just select the most effective few words or phrases. In the end what convinces is the feeling that you have taken over the arguments of those that you quote from. It is what *you* say that we are interested in, not the opinions you trot out from other people.

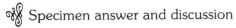 Exercise

How do we know that the various quotations come from Dennison, Monson, Booth, Clapham and Habakkuk?

 Specimen answer and discussion

To be sure in each of these cases we have to consult the footnotes. This marvellously and neatly makes clear the function of footnotes. It is the whole question of identifying information from sources, whether this information is served up in the form of a direct quotation or not, that raises the problem of scholarly apparatus.

Quite simply by scholarly apparatus we mean notes, which you will find at the foot of the page in any scholarly work, and bibliographies, which you will find at the end of scholarly books. The purpose of these footnotes and bibliographies should not be to impress you with the dazzling scholarship of the writer of the book. They are intended for use – in identifying the sources from which the author has obtained his information. Wherever there is a direct quotation in a work of scholarship there should be a footnote. More than this: wherever a particular point or idea has been derived from a source, this source should be identified in a footnote. In your own case when writing an essay there may not be a need for footnotes; but it is important that you should be aware of the principles behind the use of footnotes in scholarly books. The point is this: every now and again in reading a book, if you are reading it carefully enough, you should say to yourself: 'I wonder how he knows *that*?' The footnote should supply you with the answer.

Footnotes form one major aspect of scholarly apparatus. The other is the bibliography. In general a bibliography should serve one or other or both of two functions:

1   As a supplement to, and expansion of, footnote references, presented in systematic and orderly form. In other words it contains a full and clear statement of the sources upon which the historical work concerned is based, designed to satisfy the reader's legitimate desire to know where the author has got his information from, and as a general indication of the reliance which can be placed on the book.

2   As a guide to further reading. In the Supplementary Material booklet is the bibliography to F. M. L. Thompson's book *English Landed Society in the Nineteenth Century*.

 Exercise

1   Which of the two functions just identified does this bibliography fulfil?

2   Within Thompson's bibliography, can you distinguish between the primary sources and the secondary sources?

 Specimen answers

1   Primarily it serves the first function but it also incidentally offers guidance to further reading. We can see the immense range of primary sources he has consulted, and this confirms the impression we get from reading his book that here is a truly authoritative work properly rooted in all the available primary sources.

2   In fact, Thompson does not systematically separate primary and secondary sources, and here I would have a slight quarrel with him. But it's hard to draw firm lines. I would generally regard biographies as secondary, whereas diaries and memoirs are primary. But since some of his biographies originate from within the period he is studying, they can legitimately be regarded as primary. When we come to 'other works' matters are rather clearer. The book by Asa Briggs, and the article by W. L. Burn are clearly secondary, whereas the books or leaflets by Arnold, Bagehot (though it is a late edition), Beale, and the Duke of Bedford, to

mention just a few at the beginning, are clearly primary. I suspect that Professor Thompson has economized on and condensed his bibliography for purposes of publication. If set out in the fullest and most formal way, as appropriate for a PhD thesis, it would have been divided into two: first the primary sources, and then a second section of secondary sources.

But the main point is to see the range of sources, see the way in which a bibliography helps you to understand where a historian has got his material from, and also to see the implied hierarchy, starting with manuscript collections, then working through various types of printed sources, and ending up with the secondary sources.

2 TYPES OF HISTORICAL COMMUNICATION

I have just mentioned the slightly different requirements for a PhD thesis, which is how Thompson's work began, and a published monograph such as Thompson's book. It is possible to arrange a rough hierarchy of secondary sources (the medium, you will recall, through which historians communicate their information and interpretation), ranging from the most detailed and scholarly at the top, to those which are so popular and unscholarly that they scarcely merit the title 'secondary source' at all.

Arranged in hierarchical sequence, the types of historical communication which I propose to discuss here are:

1   *The thesis or dissertation*   Usually written by a postgraduate student for the PhD (DPhil at Oxford) degree and based almost exclusively on primary sources. This will be typed, not printed, and will usually be several hundred pages in length.

2   *The learned article*   Usually the minute examination of one particular topic, printed and published in one of the learned journals – for example, *The English Historical Review*, *The Economic History Review* or *Past and Present* – and also based on primary sources. It will usually be twenty or thirty pages in length.

3   *The scholarly monograph*   Sometimes this is the same as the PhD thesis, served up as a published book; but generally a published monograph should have a subject of greater scope and importance than the average PhD thesis; it is still based mainly on primary sources.

4   *The general history*   Self-evidently this is a very broad category. The 'general history', in whatever precise form, differs from the monograph in that it deals with a much broader topic. It differs from the text book in that it sets out to make a positive and substantial contribution to knowledge, whereas a text book basically sets out to communicate existing knowledge in as lucid a fashion as possible. The 'general history' both contains primary research and *interprets* and *synthesizes* the writings of other historians. It can incorporate all of the various sub-histories – political, economic, social – or it can concentrate on one of them.

5   *The text book*   Naturally text books can be written for a variety of different age groups and audiences. But leaving aside the more elementary books which, in any case, involve problems of educational psychology as much as history, we can regard text books covering fifth-form to university teaching as roughly in the same category.

Though all history, including text books, must in the last analysis be the historian's own interpretation, and can never be a completely objective statement of accepted knowledge, the basic task of the text book is to provide clear, simple coverage of some period or topic, in accordance with the best existing knowledge. It will draw largely on sources though the author may very probably be a primary expert in the period.

Additionally there is a type of text book devoted to the provision of extracts selected from primary sources (the source book), or excerpts from a range of secondary sources (the collection of readings). Your Course Reader is, in essence, a source book.

6 *Pop history*   History written for a wider audience is perfectly respectable provided it is written honestly, and provided it is accepted for what it is. Nowadays professional academic historians, as well as journalists, participate in the writing of pop history, the most recent form of which is best seen in the illustrated history magazines, such as Purnell's *History of the First World War*. Radio and television have provided the opportunity for a still more up-to-date form of pop history. Film, radio and television, seriously presented, can also provide a form of historical communication which comes nearer to a text book, or even to a work of general history, than it does to pop history – where the basic rationale, of course, is that it should have value as entertainment.

7 *The historical novel*   Strictly speaking this is not acceptable as a type of history – by definition, after all, it is fiction – and you should not think of the historical novel as, in any real sense, history. But there is so much confusion surrounding the question of the historical novel that it is worth glancing at it here.

Remember that a novel, whether a historical novel or not, can be a valuable primary source, but that is a different question from its role as a piece of historical communication. What one can say about the historical novel in terms of communication is that at a rather elementary level it may serve a useful purpose in arousing interest in a particular historical topic or in conveying atmosphere and background information about a particular period. It is in this sense that the novel *Gone with the Wind* has (believe it or not) been praised as having value in the teaching of history because the descriptions of the American Civil War are not only colourful but fairly reliable. But no one can really compare such passages in a novel with a serious historical study of the Civil War.

Mention of *Gone with the Wind* reminds me that the historical feature film is in many ways akin to the historical novel in that it may also arouse interest and convey a certain amount of atmosphere. The British film of the 1960s *The Charge of the Light Brigade* might possibly be regarded in this sense. But from the historian's point of view the real interest of *The Charge of the Light Brigade* is not what it tells us about the Crimean War (there are many far more reliable sources for the Crimean War) but for what it will tell the future historian about the attitudes of British film makers in the 1960s (above all an anti-heroic attitude, and a kind of detailed 'realism' – though when it came to such matters as uniforms there were many inaccuracies).

What is at issue in this attempt to classify different types of historical communication are the aims that the particular writer has in mind. There is no point in blaming someone for having written a colourful but unreliable piece of history if in fact all he or she has set out to do is to entertain or perhaps to make some money. In assessing any piece of historical writing what one must do first of all is decide what kind of history the writer is trying to produce, then judge the particular work on that basis. One is certainly entitled to be very critical of a book which has been written purely to entertain or to make money for the author, but which tries to claim that it is a genuine contribution to historical knowledge.

A valuable distinction can be made between writing history and mere bookmaking: bookmaking arises when someone feels that it would be nice to write a book without really having any very strong wish to increase knowledge or to communicate particular information; the book in fact might be about anything, it just so happens that is about an historical topic. Such books, despite the intentions, may in fact turn out to be valuable as historical communication at a fairly low level, but may on the other hand deserve our severest criticism. In general, professional historians, rightly, tend to distrust the work of someone who writes a book about the twentieth-century novel one year, and a book about Magna Carta the next year.

The main purpose of this classification is to enable you to distinguish between different types of history and to criticize them intelligently. You should thus be able to get the best out of whatever kind of history you are reading or, in the case of a film or television programme, watching.

 Exercise

Distinguish between the different types of history contained in the following list by entering the appropriate number 1–6, as defined above, in the box provided. Write down a brief comment explaining your decision.

Note that the historical novel has been excluded as *not* being a genuine type of historical writing.

A 'Whigs and Liberals in the West Riding, 1830–60', printed, about thirty pages.

B *A Social History of England 1851–1975*

C A book from which the following is the opening passage:

> There were boats on Loch Leven when John Forbes reached the narrows at Ballachulish. They lay like curled leaves on the dark water, high at the stem and stern, and almost motionless as the oarsmen pulled against the drag of the tide and the tug of the wind. They were ferrying soldiers across from Carness, and when Forbes saw the slant of pikes and the burnished barrels of muskets his memory stirred uneasily. At first there was nothing by which he could identify the soldiers, only the scarlet of their coats in the winter's grey light. Riding closer to the ferry he saw the goat's-head badge on their bonnets, the green plaids in which some of them were wrapped, and he recognized them as men of the Earl of Argyll's Regiment of Foot. When the first files waded through the shallows and formed up with their faces towards Glencoe he felt more uneasy still.

D *English Landed Society in the Nineteenth Century*

E *Mid-Victorian Britain 1851–75*

F 'The Economic and Social Background of the English Landed Interest, 1840–70', about 400 pages, typed, but not printed.

G 'Gentlemen v. Players', about thirty pages, printed.

H 'Wealth, Elites and the Class Structure of Modern Britain', about thirty pages, printed.

I *Victorian England: Aspects of English and Imperial History 1837–1901.* The opening paragraph of this book reads:

> This book makes no claim either to be comprehensive or to be based on original research. It is a general introduction to various aspects of the Victorian age, written, as far as possible, on the basis of some of the more recently-published professional works on the period.

 Answers and discussion

Passage A (2)

This is in fact the title of an article published by F. M. L. Thompson after he had completed his DPhil thesis, but before he published his book; it was published in the *English Historical Review* in 1959. The title and the length should have made it clear to you that it is a learned article.

Passage B (5)

You have an edited chapter from this book in your Supplementary Material Booklet which you have already looked at. Clearly it is a very high quality text book, and if you preferred to rate it as 4, a general history, that would not really be wrong. What I want you to get in mind are the basic distinctions between truly scholarly work founded on detailed research, more general works still of a very high order, and simple text books and popular accounts.

Passage C (6)

This is a work of popular history (John Prebble's *Glencoe*). It is extremely unlikely that some of the things the author says could have been drawn from reliable source material, for example 'his memory stirred uneasily'. Remember the question you must always keep asking when you read a work of history: 'How does he know that?'

Passage D (3)

I have just discussed this book as a scholarly monograph. It earns this title by being a work of original scholarship on a closely defined topic based almost entirely on primary sources.

Passage E (4)

Up to a point, this is also a text book, so you would not have been wrong if you had put 5. But I hope you can see that if Bédarida, covering quite a long period in his book, leans more towards being a text book, Best, taking a relatively short period and dealing with it, as it were, in depth, leans towards a specialist academic work. It is not a monograph because it is too wide ranging, and though it derives from Best's own work on primary sources, it draws mainly on other historians' work.

Passage F (1)

This, as I hope you guessed, is the original DPhil thesis which F. M. L. Thompson wrote (at Oxford) before proceeding to the further work that enabled him to fill out the thesis and produce the scholarly monograph you know about.

Passage G (2)

You may have been thrown by the title. But historians sometimes like to be lighthearted even when dealing with the most serious of topics. The author, Professor D. C. Coleman, actually has to explain in a footnote about the Gentlemen v. Players cricket match which came to an end in the early 1960s. His article really aims to refute the argument that 'gentlemanly' British industrialists were responsible for the alleged falling behind of British industry from the 1870s onwards – Coleman also contests that British industry did any worse than could be expected.

Passage H (2)

I hope that you could see that from length and specialized title this is quite definitely a learned article; it was published in *Past and Present* in 1977.

Passage I (5)

From its clear intention to provide a general introduction based on other historians' works, as well as from the rather wide title, I hope you can see that this is a text book.

3 PERIODIZATION

The past is so complex and contains such an enormous mass of material that it would not be possible for historians to deal with it at all if they did not, as it were, chop it up into convenient chunks, or periods. In fact, historians are forever dividing up the human past into periods, whether large or small. This process of periodization is fundamental to the historian's activities.

Of course this convenient habit of historians has many dangers. The past is really continuous: you do not fall asleep in a period called 'the Middle Ages' and wake up the following day to find that you are in 'the Modern World', nor even do you begin your Christmas holiday in mid-Victorian Britain and find that by the end of it you have moved into later-Victorian Britain. Periodization, the breaking up of the human past into chunks of time, is a convenience, and indeed a necessary part of the historian's endeavour to provide an intelligent and intelligible interpretation. But we must never lull ourselves into thinking of periods as having some inherent God-given truth of their own, or of having sharply defined beginnings and endings. Elementary historical text books are often characterized by a very simplistic notion of sharp breaks between different historical periods.

Since periodization forms part of an historian's interpretation, it follows that different historians will have different ideas about where period 'boundaries' should be drawn. Professor Best sees the years from 1850 to 1873 as forming a distinctive period with some sense of unity, beginning fairly sharply with the economic boom in 1850, and ending perhaps more sharply with the ending of the boom in 1873. For our purposes in this course we have established the period for our interdisciplinary study in Units 16–32 as running from 1850 to 1890. This was chosen more from the point of view of meeting the teaching needs of an interdisciplinary approach than from any profound sense on the part of the historians (like me) involved that this does form a definable, and defensible, period. From time to time, I have already suggested something of a divide into two 'sub-periods', 1850 to around 1875, and from around 1875 to 1890. But if I now give you the main chapter headings from Bédarida's entire book, you will see that he thought the past should be carved up in a slightly different way:

Part   I   The Power and the Glory: 1851–80
Part II   The Old World Resists: 1880–1914
Part III   Through Storms and Crises to Recovery: 1914–55
Part IV   A Disrupted Society: 1955–75

 Exercise

1   This list of headings brings out very neatly the way in which periodization is an act of interpretation, governed by the questions the particular historian is interested in, and by the way in which he interprets his evidence, not by some objective division into scientific categories. Briefly discuss the way in which Bédarida's periodization seems to be closely linked with definite interpretations.

2   Listed below are various passages related to the question of periodization which you might find in various kinds of historical writing. Indicate which ones you feel conform to the highest standards of historical writing (*A*), which ones you feel, given fuller explanation and qualification, are probably acceptable (*B*), and which ones you feel to be quite unacceptable (*C*). Write a short comment on each.

(a) September 1931 marked the watershed of English history between the wars. Though any division of time above a year is arbitrary, arising only from our habit of counting with arabic numerals by ten, decades take on a character of their own. What was at first merely a convenience for historians is accepted as a reality by ordinary men when they become more literate and judge the world more from books and newspapers than from their own experience. The 'twenties' and the 'thirties' were felt to be distinct periods even at the time, and September 1931 drew the line between them. The break can be defined in many ways. The end of the gold standard was the most obvious and the most immediate. Until 21 September 1931 men were hoping somehow to restore the self-operating economy which had existed, or was supposed to have existed, before 1914. After that day, they had to face conscious direction at any rate so far as money was concerned.

(b) The least disputable ground for regarding the period of years covered in this book as in some sense a unity is an economic one. These were years of unchallenged British ascendancy over the family of nations in commerce and manufactures...

The big boom begun about 1850 petered out as the Franco-Prussian war restored national rivalries to bad old intensities of truculence, and as the economic euphoria of the boom decades gave way to the relative (it was never more than relative) gloom of the so-called Great Depression; the beginning of which is precisely datable from 1873. Quite quickly, the conditions of international trade became less attractive for Britain. Prices, which had risen steadily since 1851, altered and actually began again to fall. What had, for thirty years or more, seemed regular stable markets for staple British manufactures, showed signs of saturation. Worse still, British manufacturers were now encountering what, in the fifties and early sixties, almost all of them... had been comfortably able to forget about: competition. From the United States, from Belgium, France and Germany it came. The most that Britain could hope for now, in the markets of the world, was to be *primus inter pares*: a noble and profitable position indeed, if one considered it dispassionately – but galling to businessmen who had known what it was like to have virtually no peers or rivals at all.

(c) In 1914 an old world perished. In 1918 a new one came into being.

(d) So far only a few exceptional men were conscious of this transition, but as time went on awareness of it spread, partly for reasons which we shall notice later, until it came to be generally believed that there had been great changes in or soon after the late fifteenth century in all the mutable parts of human nature. A great historian completed the idea of inventing the name 'the Renaissance', the rebirth, under which he tried to group together, as aspects of the revival of antiquity, all the revolutionary changes of those days, not only those which we have mentioned, but also others to which we have still to come. This idea, like the idea of the Middle Ages, did good service, if only in reminding historians how every department of human life is influenced by every other; but it also did harm by leading to fanciful comparisons between the naive, superstitious men of the ages of faith, whose universe seemed to them familiar and friendly, or at least accessible to conciliation by means of the Church; and the men of the Renaissance, fearless and free, asserting the rights of the individual, pouring out a defiant literature of which Man was the hero, or substituting the cold certainties of science for the comforts of religion. Such interpretations of history try to compress into a phrase and discern in a short stretch of years changes which are never alike in any two men, which are never complete in any one man, which draw their sinuous course through many generations. Continuities are never wholly broken. Many medieval habits and beliefs and institutions persisted until much later; some of them survive, but little altered, in our own time. The Renaissance was gathering force in the twelfth century, and it is still being continued by archaeologists, by grammarians, by artists, and by thinkers.

(e) Before 1850 Britain was predominantly an agricultural country; after 1850 a new age of towns and cities dawned.

(f) The mid-Victorians are characterized by their deep religious belief; with the onset of 'the Great Depression' in 1873 the age of unbelief began.

Specimen answers

1   Bédarida's very titles for his periods are interpretative: he is suggesting that there was a time of Victorian power and glory, and he sees that as running from 1851 to 1880. Then he obviously feels that there was a period of change from Victorian power and glory, but nonetheless a period in which the older ideas and their upholders ('the old world') put up a strong resistance. Then he has an

interesting title, expressing a clear interpretation, for the main part of the twentieth century, followed by another highly descriptive title for the most recent period.

2 Passage (a) A

This is a very sophisticated piece of historical writing, taken from A. J. P. Taylor's *English History 1914–1945*, which goes to some lengths to explore the philosophy underlying the idea that the twenties and the thirties are distinct periods of time.

Passage (b) B

This, as you will have realized immediately, is from Best and thus you may have felt it bound to merit an *A*. Personally, I think the notion of sharpness of change is exaggerated, even bearing in mind that Best is speaking exclusively of economic developments. It is because it is confined to economic developments that I give it a *B*. If the impression were conveyed that there was a sharp break in everything in 1873, then I think a *C* would be in order.

Passage (c) B

As it stands this is a very blunt statement, which without further explanation and qualification we would be inclined to distrust, so I would also give you full marks if you said *C*.

Clearly it contains just about as much exaggeration as is permissible in this sort of remark: pinning the perishing of the old world to one year (1914), and the coming into being of the new one also to one year (1918) is rather extreme. On the other hand what presumably lies behind the statement is the suggestion that it was really the four years of war (1914–18) that brought about this sharp change; and this is quite a reasonable suggestion to make, if we remember that in strict reality an old world can no more perish completely than an entirely new one can come into being.

Passage (d) A

Again this is an extremely subtle piece of historical writing, and once more it is outside our own Victorian 'period', taken from G. N. Clark's *Early Modern Europe*. This is a quite excellent statement of the problems involved in trying to establish exactly when 'the Renaissance' took place, the break between what we generally refer to as 'the Middle Ages' and 'the Modern World'.

Passage (e) C

This statement is just plain daft. The change from a predominantly agricultural society to an age of towns and cities could not possibly have taken place as suddenly as this.

Passage (f) C

This one is almost as daft. The switch from belief to unbelief could not possibly have taken place as suddenly as is suggested here.

The basic point to be made is that periodization is useful and indeed essential, but has many dangers and so must be approached with considerable care.

4 HISTORICAL SEMANTICS (OR HISTORICAL 'HOT POTATOES')

In stepping outside the Victorian period in that last exercise I introduced a word that you may find difficult, and about the exact meaning of which you may be puzzled: the Renaissance. This takes us into the realm of historical semantics. 'Semantics' means 'the study of the meaning of words'; there is no need to be afraid of the word, for in fact you encounter problems of semantics, changes and shifts of meaning, in your everyday use of language. Anyway, it is very important that you should appreciate the difficulties that arise in historical writing from the use of such words as 'Renaissance', 'revolution', 'romanticism', 'feudalism', 'capitalism', 'socialism', and to mention a few we have already encountered, 'liberal', 'culture' and 'class'. Every time we use one of these words we are involved in a semantic problem, that is to say a problem involving the meaning of the word.

Such words are essential in historical writing: pick up any history book and you will find dozens of them. But often they are used in such a vague, imprecise way, that instead of contributing to the communication of historical understanding they merely contribute to confusion. This is why I call them historical 'hot potatoes'.

There are six main types of such words worth noting at this stage:

1   Words that did actually exist in the periods of the past about which the historian wishes to write, but which, down through the ages, have changed in meaning. Example: 'radical'.

2   Words that have been invented to describe something in a past age, but *which were actually unknown to the people of the time*. Example: 'feudalism'.

3   Words that we use loosely in everyday speech, which, because of their vagueness, can be confusing when used in a historical context. Example: 'the people'.

4   Words used to suggest a form of periodization. Example: 'the Renaissance'.

5   Words that in the hands of some (but by no means all) historians have acquired a particular technical sense. Example: 'class', 'ideology'.

6   Most troublesome of all: words that combine a number of these problems. Examples: 'capitalism', 'imperialism', 'culture'.

Type 1   One of the most troublesome of the words that have changed in meaning is 'radical'. In strict accordance with the derivation of the word from the original Latin, a radical is someone who advocates reform 'by the roots', that is to say extreme reform. In Britain in the early nineteenth century the word was used of those who opposed the existing political system, and in fact this covered a wide range of opinions. However, the word became particularly associated with politically active middle-class figures who desired among other things: (a) as much reform in the political system as would give them the vote; (b) removal of traditional restrictions on industry and trade; and (c) reform of the antiquated legal system. In the later nineteenth century radical usually meant the more extreme members of the Liberal Party, though earlier there had been 'Tory radicals' who showed a greater interest in social questions (for example, factory reform) than did the Conservative or Tory Party in general. Radical issues, however, remained largely middle-class issues; by the early twentieth century radicalism was beginning to seem old-fashioned compared with the growth of Labour politics and socialism. Today 'radical' usually means someone who holds views of a more extreme character than those of the majority of his own political party; but to give the word any kind of precise meaning it is necessary to add a further qualifying word: hence today in Britain we have radical Christians, and the radical right – whose leadership was taken over by Margaret Thatcher.

Always remember that 'radical' is a political label describing (often somewhat vaguely) a person's political opinions, not his or her social class. An aristocrat, or a worker, could be a radical (though note, equally, that radicalism does *not* generally connote a working-class movement); if you want to identify a man by his social class or economic position, call him 'middle-class', 'a professional man', 'a banker', or whatever he is.

Type 2   The best example of the second type of problem is the word 'feudalism' (along with the adjective 'feudal' and the phrase 'feudal system'). This word was first used in the seventeenth century to describe the varied and changing social structure that existed in Europe for several centuries from about the tenth century onwards. There was never a complete 'system' in the sense of a rigid pattern of social relationships conforming to certain definite 'rules'; and, of course, the label used by later historians was quite unknown to people actually living at the time.

Yet without any doubt a social structure existed in these centuries clearly and identifiably different from the social structures of earlier or later periods. It is possible to pin down some of the essentials of feudalism with some such form of words as 'it was a system of social relationships in which inferiors held land of their superiors by virtue of performing some service for their superior; to begin with, for example, knights held land from their lords in return for performing military service'. Thus the word 'feudalism' serves a very useful purpose as a 'label' describing something which is in fact quite complicated. But since the word was not known to the people who actually lived in the period of what we call 'feudalism', clearly there are times when we must handle the word very carefully. For example, if we wish to say (and we might, provided we supplied plenty of explanation and qualification): 'The barons objected to Edward I's anti-feudal policies', we would have to remember that neither to Edward I nor to the barons could the word 'anti-feudal' have any meaning, and that, therefore, it might be better to spell out in more detail the exact nature of the policies to which the barons objected. Classical Marxism, as an approach to historical study, postulates a succession of social orders, feudalism giving way to capitalism (capitalism is discussed under heading 6).

Type 3   The example I have suggested here is 'the people'. When you find yourself using this vague word, try always to be clear exactly who you mean. Every single person in a particular country? A majority of them? All of them except the king? All of them except the rich? The working class? Quite possibly you are not really sure what you do mean, which, naturally, means that what you are writing or saying is not very good history.

Whether or not you do know what you mean, a pause for thought is called for. Almost certainly instead of the vague 'the people' you could substitute something more precise such as 'a majority of the people', 'the middle and working classes' and so on.

Another word that lends itself to the same sort of loose usage is 'the masses'.

Type 4   The problem of historical semantics joins up with the problem of periodization the moment a label is given to a particular period, as in 'The Renaissance' or 'The Enlightenment' (for the eighteenth century). One important question to ask right away is: was the label invented by men at the time, or was it a later invention of historians? Both 'The Renaissance' and 'The Enlightenment' have widespread acceptability because they are phrases that contemporaries used. In his *Lives of the Artists*, Vasari, writing in the middle of the sixteenth century, actually used the word *renascita* – rebirth or renaissance. However, for him the stress was on the *re*, the rediscovery of the best features of the ancient world, a return to something *old*. A modern historian, on the other hand, still using the word 'Renaissance' tends to lay stress on the *new* approaches developing in this period, leading to the modern world of science, of individualism, and of independent nation states.

Type 5   I have already said a fair bit about class (too much, you may well cry!), so let me concentrate on a particularly difficult word which you will encounter in your study of other disciplines and which is of vital importance in the interdisciplinary study in the second part of the course. 'Ideology', in common usage, means 'collection of attitudes and beliefs'. Thus we could speak of Whig ideology and mean 'a general belief in the crucial importance of the landed interest, tempered by a sense that it is the duty of the landed classes to give the country a lead in moving in the direction of moderate reform'; we could speak of John Stuart Mill's ideology and mean 'a commitment to individualism, with a special emphasis on such matters as the rights of women'. We might speak of Labour Party ideology, or SDP ideology, though we might have difficulty in putting down anything very precise under either heading. We might speak of public school ideology, or feminist ideology, and so on.

However, in the various forms of Marxist and Marxist-derived discourse, ideology is used in a more specific way, directly related to Marxist theory about class. Each class is seen to have its own ideology, related, though not necessarily in a simple and direct way, to its basic economic interests. In a period in which the capitalist class dominates (many Marxists would see Victorian society in these terms) the dominant ideology is capitalist, or bourgeois ideology. Many phenomena which others might see as on the whole desirable, such as parliamentary institutions or novels with elements of social criticism in them, are seen as essentially products of bourgeois ideology. One might then speak of an 'alternative ideology' of a non-dominant, but perhaps 'rising' class – for example, the working class.

Personally, I use ideology in the first sense but when you encounter the word, or wish to use it yourself, always be absolutely clear which sense is intended.

Type 6   Some of the words most commonly used by historians combine two or more of the problems listed above. Words such as capitalism and imperialism have both changed their meaning in general usage, and have acquired special technical meanings. The Victorians used the word 'capitalist' in a fairly neutral way simply to mean owner or employer. And many historians would use the word 'capitalism' in a neutral way to describe a type of economic organization in which the most important persons are the owners of the capital upon which commerce and industry is based. But since Marxism, in its classical form, postulates that the system of capitalism will be superseded by one of socialism, and argues that capitalism inevitably involves the exploitation of the workers, the term then acquires hostile overtones. Many non-Marxist historians would contest the idea of there having been a feudal order which is then superseded by a capitalist order, arguing that strong elements of capitalism can be found very far back in the human past.

Imperialism, in its most simple meaning, means the extension of the power of a single-nation state over other states so as to establish an empire. The word first came into general use in Britain to describe the aggressive policies pursued by Napoleon III (we met him in connection with the Crimean War) in the 1850s. It remained a term of abuse when radicals and liberals used it of Disraeli's policies in the 1870s. However, by the 1880s the word had become respectable and a number of politicians and publicists were proud to announce themselves as imperialists. Some historians would confine the use of imperialism to that aggressive expansion of the European world into the Third World which took place from the later nineteenth century onwards; others would say that elements of imperialism have been apparent in all ages. Marxists see imperialism as a particular stage in the development of capitalism.

Perhaps most difficult and dangerous of all is the word 'culture'. One of the most important topics in the second part of this course is entitled 'Culture: Production, Consumption and Status'; throughout the first part of the course, in the various introductions to the disciplines, you will find it being argued that various forms of literature, art, music and philosophy are 'culturally constructed'.

In the phrase 'culturally constructed', 'culture' is being used in the anthropological sense of the total network of human activities in a given society, including economic and social structure, religious beliefs, customs and habits, and so on.

A painting, or a symphony, is said to be 'culturally constructed'. What is meant is that rather than being the product of the artist's independent genius, it is really a product of the whole network of influences operating in the artist's society. The difficulty is that some academics see these influences as going back for centuries so that, for instance, Greek traditions could be seen as part of nineteenth-century culture, while others see cultures changing as economic structures change, so that nineteenth-century industrial culture is seen as constructing rather different art forms from eighteenth-century non-industrial culture. My own view, for what it is worth, is that it is proper to speak of literary and artistic artefacts as being 'culturally constructed', if we have this long-term scale and multiplicity of influences in mind, but wrong to see them as simply determined by the particular immediate age in which they were created. However, as will emerge during the course, that is a matter for legitimate debate. What I want to stress first of all is this very important anthropological meaning of culture with which you may not be very familiar, that is 'the total network of human activities in a given society'.

Possibly the definition you are most familiar with is something like: 'the best artistic and intellectual products and activities in a given society', 'best' implying what is sometimes referred to as 'high culture', that is to say opera, 'classical' music, 'serious' literature, and so on. However, there is an intermediate sense which has come increasingly into use, as when we speak of 'popular culture': here we are including in the term 'all the artistic, intellectual and creative products and activities in a given society', including popular music and folksongs, the popular press, sports, fairs and popular entertainments of all sorts.

So, to recapitulate, the three main definitions of 'culture' are:

1   The total network of human activities and value systems in a given society (as in 'Western culture', 'Oriental culture', 'Tudor culture' and 'Victorian culture').

2   All the artistic and intellectual products and activities in a given society.

3   The 'best' artistic and intellectual products and activities in a given society (for example, 'high' art, 'classical' music, 'serious' literature).

The first definition is the one you will most usually encounter during the first part of this course. The third definition is the one the Victorians usually had in mind when they spoke of 'culture'. In the second part of the course there will be a further discussion of definitions, and a particular emphasis on culture in the second sense.

When you write a history essay you will find that you have to make use of the words discussed above, or others like them. Each time you must be absolutely clear in your own mind what meaning lies behind the phrases you use. There is no point talking about 'the radicals' or about 'capitalism' unless you know what, in terms of real historical people, real events and real processes, these phrases signify. Too often, of course, students (and others!) use phrases like these because they think they sound good, without really being clear about their meaning. Remember: if you don't know what you mean, whoever is reading your work won't know what you mean either. Always consider: what would you say if asked what it means.

 Exercise

Turn to Bédarida's chapter 'The Crisis of Victorian Values' in the Supplementary Material booklet. In the section titled '*Laissez-faire* challenged', read from the paragraph beginning 'So the intellectual foundations of *laissez-faire*...' to the end of the section. Note down all the words that give rise to problems of historical semantics. If you feel able to, add a comment about what you understand the word to mean, or even about the various different meanings which you believe the word can have. But if this sounds impossibly difficult don't worry about it; the important point is to identify these historical hot potatoes.

✺ Specimen answer and discussion

Laissez-faire   Perhaps you know this word as a rough synonym for private enterprise. The phrase (French, of course) was first used in the eighteenth century to describe a policy of freeing a country from the economic restrictions which had been characteristic of the mediaeval and early modern periods. It came into general usage in Britain in the nineteenth century to characterize a particular type of social and economic policy which insisted that it was best for the government not to interfere in social and economic matters but to leave such matters to the free operation of private enterprise and the demands of the market.

Economic individualism   Essentially this is just another way of saying *laissez-faire*. (Note that in ordinary speech we use individualism in a rather different way as referring to a person who prefers to go his or her own way.)

Ideological   Although as a historian Bédarida is strongly influenced by Marxism, the usage here, I think, is the wide one rather than the purely technical Marxist one.

The State   With a capital S like this, what is meant is the government in all its aspects.

Interventionism   This means action by the government in economic and social matters, and is thus a departure from *laissez-faire*.

Radical   This is radical in the strictly Victorian sense, as in connection with someone like Joseph Chamberlain whose speech on municipal interventionism is in the Course Reader extract VI.5.

Nationalization   This means the take-over of major sectors of the economy by the State.

Collective management   This means management by the State on behalf of the community as a whole. Another word sometimes used with this meaning is 'collectivism'.

Socialist   Broadly, in this context, Bédarida is using the word 'socialist' simply, as is stated, to mean advocacy of nationalization and collective management. The general meaning of 'someone who wishes to change society in the direction of greater equality through action by the state' is clear enough. But within that broad definition there are many types of socialist, from those who advocate the complete overthrow of the capitalist system, to those who advocate gradual social reform in the manner of the Labour Party under Clement Attlee.

Ultra-individualist   Obviously an extreme supporter of *laissez-faire* and opponent of any intervention by the state.

Liberalism   Here we have a very good example of the ambiguity of the word; Dicey clearly saw liberalism as connoting unrestricted freedom (for the rich to do what they liked, for the poor to starve in peace) and minimal government action; but other liberals, and this was increasingly so in the later-Victorian period, saw themselves as proponents of positive reform.

Socialism   Again Bédarida has a general definition in mind embracing the various brands, that is to say the movement in favour of greater state action on behalf of the less privileged members of society.

Classical liberalism   That is to say the liberalism of Dicey and, in large measure, John Stuart Mill.

Ideological   Again the general, non-technical meaning, is implied.

Intelligentsia   This word has continental origins and is relatively unfamiliar in English (remember Bédarida is French): he means the 'intellectuals', all those who think and write about politics and the problems of society – Mill, Dicey (who wrote a famous book about the passing of classical liberalism), Matthew Arnold, Marx, are all examples.

Discussion

That's a rather high count of hot potatoes for two abbreviated paragraphs, and characteristic of Bédarida's slightly abstract style. Best, I think you will have found, is less prone to make frequent use of these difficult words, but the fact is in historical writing they simply cannot be avoided.

You may also have noted down the following phrases:

Moloch State   This is a biblical metaphor, rather than a piece of historical semantics. Moloch was the Canaanite idol to whom children were sacrificed, and has entered into the language in the metaphorical sense of 'a cruel power to which sacrifice is made': this gives you a very clear idea of the views of Dicey and his like towards active government and insight into their hatred of socialism.

Rationalism   This is not a specifically historical word; in general usage it means action governed by reason.

Marxist Socialism, Social-Democratic Federation, Fabian Socialism, Fabian Society, religious socialism, Christian socialism, Independent Labour Party   These are all either precise brands of socialism, or exact titles of socialist groups or parties, so they don't really raise any problems of meaning.

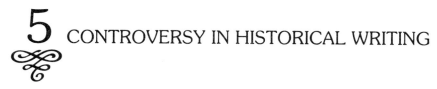

5 CONTROVERSY IN HISTORICAL WRITING

There are many famous controversies in history. 'Why did the American colonists rebel against the British Government?' 'What exactly was the Renaissance and when did it take place?' 'Did the Industrial Revolution raise or lower the standard of living of the majority of the British people?' 'What were the causes of the English Civil War in the seventeenth century?' 'What were the causes of the Second World War in the twentieth century?' 'Who killed the Princes in the Tower?'

Historians do disagree with each other. But then so, sometimes, do scientists. We must accept that all historical writing is in the end *interpretation*, that it must contain a subjective element. But this does not mean that 'one opinion is as good as another'. When you are reading history you must always be on guard against the crank or charlatan who claims to be putting forward a startling and imaginative new interpretation. If he has not observed the principles of scholarship outlined in this three-week *Introduction to History*, then you have every right to reject his claims.

Similarly with your own writing. Imagination, the ability to penetrate behind the facts to the connections between them, is expected of you in any essay you write in the arts, but in a history essay you must be guided first of all by the information you have acquired from your various sources. There is all the difference in the world between creative historical *imagination* and sheer *invention* (that is, in this connection, simply making things up). Now, I know that Foundation Course students feel (very reasonably) that they do not have sufficient background knowledge to do other than follow the lines presented in their course units and set reading. We would not expect you to take a highly original line (and, frankly, would not usually welcome it), but do always try to be critical in your reading, and to use imagination (but not invention!) in your interpretations.

Nevertheless two students, equally conscientious, equally able, may write entirely different essays on the same subject. Yet if both students have observed the basic principles of historical writing, both essays may be equally good. (It should be added that at student level the probability is that one essay will be more in accordance with historical reality as accepted by the leading historical authorities, and thus better as history.) Two historians, equally scholarly, may also present different conclusions on the same subject. From what has been said in earlier sections the reasons for this should be clear to you.

 Exercise

See how many of these reasons you can now recall.

 Specimen answer

1   History is always in some sense 'a dialogue between present and past' – every age rewrites history to take account of its own current preoccupations – thus a historian writing in 1987 will tend to present a different account from a historian writing in 1927.

2   The individual historian may give greater or lesser weight to a particular theory which leads to interpreting the evidence in a particular way.

3   Greater or lesser use of modern 'scientific' techniques, for example statistics, can yield different conclusions.

4   The primary sources upon which history is based are usually fragmentary and imperfect and frequently conflict with each other so that historians studying the same evidence can still genuinely arrive at conflicting conclusions.

To these four you may perhaps have thought of adding this further reason:

5   Political differences. A Conservative, for example, might wish to interpret the mid-Victorian period as a time of general social harmony in which conditions are generally getting better for everyone, whereas a socialist might prefer to direct attention to the many examples of extreme misery, and also to instances of tension between employers and employees.

Among these five reasons for the existence of controversy and disagreement in historical writing, some historians would stress some more than others. Personally, I do not think political views play a very strong part. However, I must stress that this is a *personal* view. If you disagree (and it's a point well worth thinking about and discussing with fellow students) you are in good company. Many would argue that political judgements (in the widest sense, to include, say, feminism, rather than merely party political stances) are bound to affect one's historical interpretation. My own view, to repeat, is that the really good historian should be able to surmount his or her political outlook – though no doubt there will always remain differences of emphasis related to political conviction. I would stress above all the fragmentary nature of historical sources which often makes conclusive answers to particular problems very difficult.

Two final reflections on the reasons for historical controversy. Sometimes historians do express their interpretation of a particular subject in rather more extreme terms than their own reading of the evidence would really allow for; there is, let us say, a natural tendency to make one's own point of view stand out as strongly as possible in contrast to one's predecessors and opponents. Likewise historians sometimes also form a personal emotional attachment to their own side of the argument – and so find it difficult to see the other point of view.

Controversy is a strong word. It implies more than just differences of interpretation among various historians. Rather it suggests that there are two or more schools of thought ranged against each other over the interpretation of a particular historical episode.

Disagreement and different opinions, we have seen, are inevitable. But should not historians play down their differences, instead of indulging in vigorous controversy of a type which sometimes verges upon personal attack?

In fact argument and debate, properly conducted, serve valuable purposes in all academic disciplines, history included.

 Exercise

Have you any idea what these purposes might be? If you genuinely have no idea, don't rack your brains, but go straight on to my answer.

 Specimen answer

1   Controversy can open up new lines of enquiry. The historian who has researched deeply into some problem can become blinded to the existence of wider perspectives and alternative lines of enquiry as she delves ever deeper into her subject. If her interpretations are attacked boldly by other historians, then she will be forced to defend herself and to give consideration to the alternative interpretations forced upon her in the controversy. Out of all this the total sum of historical knowledge may be increased significantly.

2   It can lead to the critical testing of a particular generalization or hypothesis. Just as the detailed researcher can become blinded by his researches, so too the historian who has formulated sweeping generalizations or bold hypotheses can fall in love with his own theories and forget that every general formulation must be constantly re-examined in the light of new evidence. Controversy with another historian will force him to undertake this re-examination. Again the cause of historical knowledge may be advanced.

3   It can lead to new synthesis. An historical controversy may take the form of one hypothesis being posed against another. It may be that the historians concerned dig in their heels and refuse to modify their own hypotheses. Even so, a clear sharp statement of the conflicting theories may make it possible for other historians to present a *synthesis* which combines the best of each hypothesis, and in fact marks a definite advance in historical knowledge.

 Exercise

One of the most intense controversies which has continued to rage over the Victorian period is that concerning the performance of British entrepreneurs (or businessmen or industrialists – in this context the words mean basically the same thing) from the 1870s onwards, concentrating on the issue of whether Britain's relatively poor economic performance in relation to the rest of the world compared with that of the mid-Victorian boom was caused by the inadequacies of British industrialists. Among the points made in this debate were the following:

1   the sociological or cultural ('culture' here being used in the sense of the first definition given in the previous section) argument that, lulled into complacency by Britain's supremacy during the mid-Victorian boom, the later generation of entrepreneurs preferred the life of cultured ('culture' in our third definition!), gentlemanly pursuits, and the countryside, to the hard work of sponsoring new investments and new technological developments;

2   (often linked with the previous one) the argument that Britain was deficient in technological education, and that businessmen in general had a distrust of scientists;

3   the counter-argument that British industrialists were as efficient and enterprising as their foreign competitors;

4   the argument that whatever deficiencies there may have been, they were not because of sociological and cultural factors;

5   (usually linked to this) the argument that acting on the basis of a rational judgement of their own interests, late-Victorian entrepreneurs acted vigorously and efficiently;

6   the argument that the main reason for a failure in export markets was the high tariff barriers which foreign countries erected against British exports;

7   the argument that it is impossible to generalize about the performance of British entrepreneurs, some in fact performing very well, some performing not so well.

Now these different arguments are advanced in one or more of the following passages. I want you to allocate each passage to the main argument (1–7) that it is advancing.

(a)   Before the twentieth century the average British businessman was not a 'gentleman' and never became either a knight, a peer, or even the owner of a country house... Sociologically, the incentive to make money fast was by no means weak in Victorian Britain, the attraction of the gentry and aristocracy by no means overwhelming, especially not to the cohorts of middle-class conscious and often non-conformist (i.e. deliberately anti-aristocratic) Northerners and Midlanders, their heads filled with mottos like 'where there's muck there's brass', and solid pride in their productive achievements. They were proud of the soot and smoke in which they drenched the cities in which they made their money... Simple sociological explanations therefore will not do. In any case, economic explanations of economic phenomena are to be preferred if they are available. There are indeed several, all resting tacitly or openly on the assumption that in a capitalist economy (at all events in its nineteenth-century versions) businessmen will be dynamic only insofar as this is rational by the criterion of the individual firm, which is to maximise its gains, minimise its losses, or possibly merely to maintain what it regards as a satisfactory long-term rate of profit. But since the rationality of the individual firm is inadequate, this may not work out to the best advantage of the economy as a whole, or even of the individual firm. (Hobsbawm, *Industry and Empire*)

(b)   Few beliefs are so well-established in the credo of British economic history as the belief that the late Victorians failed...

[There follows several pages of mathematical analysis]

... There is, indeed, little left of the dismal picture of British failure painted by historians. The alternative is a picture of an economy not stagnating but growing as rapidly as permitted by the growth of its resources and the effect of exploitation of the available technology. (McCloskey, 'Did Victorian Britain fail?')

(c)   ... the Britain of the late nineteenth century basked complacently in the sunset of economic hegemony. In many firms, the grandfather who started the business and built it by unremitting application and by thrift bordering on miserliness had long died; the father who took over a solid enterprise and, starting with larger ambitions, raised it to undreamt-of heights, and passed on the reins; now it was the turn of the third generation, the children of affluence, tired of the tedium of trade and flushed with the bucolic aspirations of the country gentleman. (One might more accurately speak of 'shirt sleeves to hunting jacket – or dress coat, or ermine robes – in three generations'.) Many of them retired and forced the conversion of their firms into joint-stock companies. Others stayed on and went through the motions of entrepreneurship between the long weekends; they worked at play and played at work. (Landes, *The Unbound Prometheus*)

(d)   By education we really mean the imparting of four kinds of knowledge, each with its own contribution to make to economic performance:

(1) the ability to read, write, and calculate;

(2) the working skills of the craftsman and mechanic;

(3) the engineer's combination of scientific principle and applied training; and

(4) high-level scientific knowledge, theoretical and applied.

In all four areas, Germany represented the best that Europe had to offer; in all four, with the possible exception of the second, Britain fell far behind. (Landes, *The Unbound Prometheus*)

(e)   If innovations do not yield reductions in average unit costs, then it would be irrational for a businessman to introduce them even if the innovations would benefit the future growth of the economy. The individual businessman cannot be expected to estimate external economies. The net social returns from investment in innovations may be higher than the private returns, with the result that a capitalistic environment may produce a rate of innovation well below the social optimum. (Richardson, 'Chemicals', p. 275)

(f)   Can we still continue to generalize with such certainty about the characteristics of 'the British entrepreneur' between 1870 and 1914? It is not simply that as *between* industries, British entrepreneurial performace was 'patchy' and that a patchiness existed in 'old' industries as well as 'new', but that *within* industries (e.g. engineering, iron and steel, glass, wool textiles) there existed marked differences in performance between different sections, between different firms. And if the diversity of experience appears even stronger than has hitherto been conceded, can we continue to accept generalized explanations about characteristics which, insofar as they amounted to 'shortcomings' or even 'failure', were so variously distributed. (Sigsworth, 'Some problems in business history')

(g)   Thus, in a variety of ways, the new urban and industrial society that was Britain moved towards a new and different economy. It was in large measure the economy men wanted, an economy that supplied their needs abundantly and on the whole efficiently. It was able to do this because capital and enterprise themselves responded in these years to the prospects offered by the main demand for consumer (and other) goods in a context of rising real incomes.

To the armchair critics who demanded to know why the old exporting industries did not introduce technological improvements to reduce costs and raise productivity, the industrialist might not unreasonably have replied with a counter-question. What good would it have done where tariff walls were everywhere rising to keep his products out, however they were priced? Even the most vigorous of the new men in consumer industries (like soap) found that exporting was doomed. (Wilson, 'Economy and sociology in late Victorian Britain')

(h)   Although foreign competition exposed certain weaknesses in British industry it would certainly be wrong to conclude that British industrialists as a whole were less efficient or less enterprising than their foreign counterparts. Some industrial sectors, notably shipping and boots and shoes and certain branches of the glass and woollen industries, showed remarkable powers of resiliency in this period. Likewise certain branches of the iron and steel, chemical and engineering industries were prepared to adapt to changed conditions. Some of the developments in the heavy engineering sector, especially in ring spinning machinery, steam engines and heavy machine tools hardly convey the impression that manufacturers were unwilling to accept changes. Moreover, the fact that some industrialists were slow to adopt new techniques does not necessarily mean that they were inefficient or lacked enterprise. One might, for example, criticize cotton manufacturers on the grounds that they ignored the ring spindle and automatic loom. But this was not due to conservatism on their part but rather to the fact that the new machinery was not really suitable to English conditions of manufacture. (Aldcroft, *The Development of British Industry and Foreign Competition 1875–1914*)

Specimen answers and discussion

1 (c)   2 (d)   3 (b) (h)   4 (a)   5 (a) (e)   6 (g)   7 (f)

If you haven't got these answers, go back and read carefully through the extracts again. Passage (a) actually covers two points, the second one being repeated in passage (e). A strong defence of industrialists is contained in both (b) and (h).

Exercise

Now read this extract from a recent book, and briefly note down what argument it is making.

... the later nineteenth century saw the consolidation of a national élite that, by virtue of its power and prestige, played a central role both in Britain's modern achievements and its failures. It administered the most extensive empire in human history with reasonable effectiveness and humanity, and it maintained a remarkable degree of political and social stability at home while presiding over a redistribution of power and an expansion of equality and security. It also presided over the steady and continued erosion of the nation's economic position in the world. The standards of value of this new élite of civil servants, professionals, financiers, and landed proprietors, inculcated by a common education in public schools and ancient universities and reflected in the literary culture it patronized, permeated by their prestige much of British society beyond the élite itself. These standards did little to support, and much to discourage, economic dynamism. They threw earlier enthusiasms for technology into disrepute, emphasized the social evils brought by the industrial revolution, directed attention to issues of the 'quality of life' in preference to the quantitative concerns of production and expansion and disparaged the restlessness and acquisitiveness of industrial capitalism.

 Specimen answer

This is the cultural or sociological argument about industrialists turning towards gentlemanly pursuits.

There may be various reasons lying behind the different views presented in these extracts. Many of the historians who were strongly critical of British entrepreneurs drew much of their evidence from reports sent back by British consulates in various foreign countries: these reports tended to stress the failures of British businessmen to market their goods effectively. However, perhaps this was a rather one-sided source. McCloskey, in his defence of British entrepreneurs, makes much use of sophisticated statistical and mathematical techniques. Hobsbawm is a leading Marxist historian.

   Yet in the end my feeling is that fundamental disagreement is not as great as it might appear. We seem really to be dealing with a difference of emphasis, and that's usually the way it is in historical controversy. It is worth noting that extract (h), which seems to be a strong defence of British entrepreneurs, is followed in the original book by a sentence which reads: 'On the other hand neither must one adopt an unduly complacent attitude when discussing the performance of British business in this period.'

 Exercise

I have argued that historical controversy helps to clarify issues, helps one to arrive at a new synthesis. Now you write a brief paragraph on British industry and British entrepreneurs in the later Victorian period, trying to bring out the best of the points made in the various different extracts.

 Specimen answer

It is impossible to characterize all entrepreneurs as efficient or inefficient: there was great variation not just from industry to industry, but within industries. While it may be true that some industrialists sought the gentlemanly life of the élite, many had small businesses in the North and Midlands, were dedicated to making money, and had a strong interest in technological innovation. No doubt, they paid greater attention to their own immediate profits than to the national interest, and thus their activities may well not have best served the needs of the British economy as a whole. This weakness was aggravated by the generally low level of technological education in Britain and perhaps also by a lack of interest among businessmen in science. Much of the failure to win overseas markets was a result of the imposition of tariff barriers by foreign countries.

 Discussion

I am sure you wrote something totally different from that, but I hope you can see from my answer the way in which one can put together a balanced, level-headed account which recognizes that in a world-wide perspective British industry was doing less well from the 1870s onwards, but that simplistic general denunciations of British entrepreneurs are inappropriate.

6 HISTORY AND THE OTHER ARTS DISCIPLINES

This is an arts course, and these units, *Introduction to History*, form only a part of that course. In addressing many major problems (for example, the role of government in sponsoring the arts, the place of the arts in a university education, the nature of cultural change in, say, the 1960s, or the 1980s, or the 1880s, improving the quality of life, or the rights of women), the tools and insights of one single discipline will never be enough for a really thorough analysis. Furthermore it is one of the major aims spelled out for this Foundation Course 'to raise questions about the relationships between the arts and society'.

Historians are drawn naturally into a form of interdisciplinary study and into raising such questions.

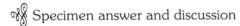 Exercise

We have already seen one way in which historians are brought directly into contact with art, literature, and so on. Say what this is; then try to see how historians in their normal task of enquiring into the human past and attempting to produce an interpretation or reconstruction of it become further involved in art, literature, and so on.

Specimen answer and discussion

We have already seen (Unit 2, section 4) the use historians make of literature and art as primary sources.

If you got that, well done! To go further (which you may well have found impossible) is to really look more closely at *why* such sources should be of use to historians. I would put it something like this: if historians are to understand a past age totally and thoroughly then they must understand the thoughts, the creative activities, the artistic objectives, and so on, of the age; beyond that, if historians are to make some kind of evaluation of the achievements of a particular age (as I asked you to do in the exercise at the very end of Unit 2) they must, of course, consider the art, literature, philosophy, music, as well as the science, technology, political institutions, welfare provisions, and so on, of the age (I am using 'age' in a slightly unsatisfactory, everyday, metaphorical way – what I really mean, of course, is 'a particular society during a particular period of time').

That has been to look at how historians bring in material from the other arts disciplines. Let us look now at the way in which history in itself is essential in the study of art, literature, music and philosophy.

 Exercise

You may, very reasonably, have no thoughts on this one at all (in which case go straight to my answer and discussion). But just pause for a moment or two to see if you can think of the two main ways in which history is invaluable to these other disciplines.

Specimen answer

I would argue that history is invaluable in:

1   helping our full *understanding* and *appreciation* of a painting, poem, symphony, and so on, because history tells us about the society in which the work of art was produced;

2   assisting in the problem of *explaining* how a particular piece of art, literature, or whatever, came to be produced.

What I am saying, essentially, is that the study of history helps us to establish what can best be termed the *historical* or *social context* for works of art or literature.

To try to clinch the point, let us look at some comparisons and contrasts between various famous literary, artistic and musical figures. Some you may be very familiar with, others not at all; but work through the next exercise anyway since (like most of my exercises) this is developing a point as well as getting you thinking.

1   There are some obvious differences between the poems of Chaucer and the poems of Robert Burns. Why?

2   There are some obvious differences between the novels of Jane Austen, Charles Dickens, George Eliot (Mary Anne Evans) and Thomas Hardy. Why?

3   There are some obvious differences between the paintings of the Pre-Raphaelites and those of Picasso. Why?

4   There are some obvious differences between the symphonies of Mozart and those of Beethoven. Why?

5   There are (I am sure you will believe!) some obvious differences between the poems and plays which I once used to try to write, and those of William Shakespeare. Why?

I suggest you start off with this last one, then work your way through questions 1–4.

 Specimen answers and discussion

5   The obvious answer here, I think, would have to be that while Shakespeare was a genius, I personally had no talent whatsoever for writing poems or plays; in this case all more complex or more historical explanations pale into insignificance. This is an extreme case, of course, but I do not think we should ever leave the question of individual talent or individual genius out of the reckoning altogether.

1   The simple answer, I would have thought, is that Chaucer lived in the Middle Ages, wrote in Middle English about mediaeval people and, while dealing with many enduring facets of human nature, dealt with some specifically mediaeval activities, for example, the Pilgrimage to Canterbury; Burns, however, by contrast, was writing in the later eighteenth century, mainly in a particular Scottish rural context.

2   You might well have first wanted to make the point that Jane Austen and George Eliot were both women. Any historical answer within a couple of lines must necessarily be very superficial, but what I had in mind was that Jane Austen was writing at the very beginning of the nineteenth century, when many parts of the country were totally unaffected by industrialization and when the social imperatives were those of an estate (not class) society; most of Dickens's works date from the mid-Victorian period which we have discussed in at least some detail, while George Eliot and Thomas Hardy were writing in the late-Victorian period – so far we have scarcely *proved* that there are substantial changes in attitudes and values between the mid-Victorian period and the late-Victorian period, but at least that is the sort of historical question which would arise in comparing Dickens with the two later authors.

3   I presume what one would say here is that Picasso belongs to the modern age in which naturalism, exact representation, is no longer a characteristic of painting, whereas the Pre-Raphaelites belong not only to a highly naturalistic phase but to one in which religious influences were very strong.

4   I don't know how you might have reacted to this one. I put it in because I want to signal ahead to something you will encounter in Units 7–9 *Introduction to Music*. There you will learn that at the time of Beethoven a new type of symphony came into existence which, quite plausibly, can be fairly directly linked to the emergence of a kind of non-aristocratic audience in public concert halls, and indirectly to commercialization, industrialization and changes in the social structure. Within such a broad definition of change one would have to include

such things as changes in the technology of musical instruments, and new currents of literary and political thinking. But after that there might well be scope for a discussion of the particular personalities, talents and genius of the two composers.

All I want to stress is that there is no escape from consideration of the historical context. In philosophy, as you will learn in Units 13–15 *Introduction to Philosophy*, there is some relationship between the great social and economic upheavals in the seventeenth century, involving the break-up of many of the remaining elements of the feudal order, and the turning of philosophers to questions of man's freedom of choice – something earlier philosophers had not preoccupied themselves with; so too between industrialization, the growth of towns and new social problems at the end of the eighteenth century and on in to the nineteenth century, and the turning of philosophers to questions of social organization and social morality.

As it happens, one usually has little need these days to persuade colleagues in other arts disciplines of the importance of the historical context. In the last decade or two the emphasis has very much swung towards studying works of art from the point of view of how they were produced, who consumes them, and what their relationship is to the culture (in our first, anthropological, definition) or society from which they have sprung. As already noted, it is now widely asserted that any such work is necessarily 'culturally constructed'. Indeed the function of historians has now perhaps become that of insisting upon the complexities of the interrelationships between art and society. In looking historically at any work of art, many historians would argue, it can be useful to distinguish between the following words or phrases:

'*Culture*', as in the phrase 'culturally constructed', which arguably may need to be seen as extending over many centuries as, for instance, when ideals of the ancient Greeks or of the Renaissance are still influential in Victorian times;

'*Historical context*', that is the immediate 'period', though as we have seen (Unit 3, section 3) periodization is very far from being an exact science;

'*Referential elements*': what I have in mind is that apart from the question of a work of art being shaped basically by culture and the historical context, it may contain within it references to actual occurrences or people of the time, significant or insignificant, as when *Hard Times* refers to a strike, or the Pre-Raphaelites include representations of each other in their paintings;

Finally a range of more or less '*autonomous*' elements (that is, more or less independent of the wider culture or the historical context), ranging from modes of expression ('classical' and 'romantic' traditions existed in the Victorian period, though ultimately, of course, each arises from culture and history) to purely personal predilections and idiosyncracies, and perhaps even personal circumstances. (Where, if anywhere, do we put the fact of Beethoven's deafness in his later years? Being male or female may well be of considerable importance, but then that has to be related to the way in which males and females are treated within a particular historical context.)

I do not wish you to master or memorize this material: I simply want to make two fundamental points.

1   History is vitally important in its relationship with the other arts subjects.

2   That relationship is not a simple one. Just to get at the basics again, another exercise.

 Exercise

Could *Hard Times* have been written a hundred years earlier (in 1754) or a hundred years later (in 1954)? Write your answer down now, but before I give my answer, let me discuss another similar question.

The question I want to discuss is that of the Great Exhibition of 1851, mentioned occasionally by Best, and the subject of a detailed study in Unit 16. Among other things it comprised a striking piece of architecture (the 'Crystal Palace'), various more or less 'artistic' exhibits, and many fine examples of technological innovation. Could the Great Exhibition have been held a hundred years earlier, or a hundred years later? Well, clearly the exhibits would have been very different at both times, and in 1751 neither the technological exhibits, nor the technology to build the 'Crystal Palace' would have been available; more than that, the whole idea of such an exhibition was a product of Victorian optimism and assertiveness, and would have been quite alien to the ideas prevalent in 1751. However, and perhaps you have anticipated my line of thought here, there was actually a 'great exhibition' in 1951, the Festival of Britain. Here we have an interesting example of what might be termed a long-term cultural influence: 1951 was deliberately chosen as being exactly a hundred years after the first Great Exhibition; the immediate historical context, of course, was the wish to demonstrate Britain's triumphant recovery from the Second World War.

 Specimen answer and discussion

I hope some of the following thoughts occurred to you.

Within a smaller population there was at least as much relative poverty and deprivation in 1751 as in 1851, so one could certainly write about 'hard times', literally understood; generally matters were much better in 1951, but undoubtedly 'hard times' still existed for many people. But the particular sort of early industrial society Dickens is describing existed neither in 1751 nor in 1951. Undoubtedly the message about the inferiority of 'mechanical' methods of instruction, the insistence on mere facts, as against more sensitive approaches would be applicable in 1751 as in 1951; but the specific reference is to currents of thought which were at their strongest in the early nineteenth century. One could add that the novel as an art form was only coming into existence in 1751, and was already being transformed by 1951. However, a sensible answer might be that a work of literature termed *Hard Times* could have been published in 1751 as in 1951, and could have made many of the same points; but in style and content it would obviously have been very different, and in very different ways, at both dates.

I have been looking at history in its relationship with other disciplines. I now want briefly to make the point that in studying history seriously one does many of the same sorts of things that one does in studying literature, music, art and philosophy. Above all, in all arts subjects one does not just memorize a lot of second-hand information, one directly studies *texts*, whether these be historical documents, poems, pieces of music, or whatever. In studying (or *reading*, in the jargon of today) these texts, one has to:

1   decide what category they fall into (act of parliament or private diary, novel or poem, symphony or sonata);

2   *understand* what is in them;

3   apply principles of *criticism* (these vary from discipline to discipline; I have been concerned with the principles of historical source criticism);

4   follow up references and allusions in the text (for history, this formed part of the list of questions I gave in connection with the principles of historical source criticism).

Of course, there are important differences between studying history and studying the other arts disciplines. However much art historians or musicologists, for example, may be concerned with the way in which art or music is produced and consumed, and with its relationship to the surrounding culture, there must be questions about whether a particular composer is 'great' or not, or whether a particular painting is a 'masterpiece' or not, even if it is insisted that these terms in the end are 'culturally constructed'. No one would ever claim that the sort of document historians mainly deal with was 'great' or a 'masterpiece'. Mrs Beeton's *Book of Household Management* is a considerable achievement, one has great respect for those who drafted the *Summons to the Trades Union Congress of*

1868, and one may even find enjoyment in the literary style of Macaulay's speech of 1852; but one would not compare any of these documents with a poem by a major poet or a painting by a major artist. In fact, in the other arts subjects there is much of value in studying one single painting or listening to one piece of music, or analysing one short piece of philosophical exposition. In history, I do ask you to study single documents, but this is merely as an exercise in historical methods. You cannot learn much history from one document. The whole essence of historical study lies in the putting together of a large number of documents to build up a complete interpretation. History, after all, is concerned with a vast range of human activities within society. It is concerned with public events, relationships between groups and society, changes in these relationships, and with questions of causes, consequences and interrelationships over a wide field of social activities.

Yet these activities invite our admiration and move our emotions, as do great art, great music and great literature. There is indeed much to admire in the creation of political and social institutions, in the building of cities and transport systems, as in the creation of cathedrals, paintings and novels; and as also in the struggle of the underprivileged against oppression, and of individuals and groups in all walks of society against man's inhumanity to man. History joins with the other arts disciplines in being both the celebration, and the rigorous analysis and criticism, of human activities and human achievements.

7 REMINDING YOU OF THE 'ESSENTIAL FEATURES' OF VICTORIAN SOCIETY

You won't have time now to study further the documents in your Course Reader. But I would like just to remind you again of my six headings and to indicate how some of the documents, which I hope you will take the opportunity of reading at some stage, relate to these headings. No document, of course, can ever be tied conclusively to any one 'heading'. A document's usefulness always depends upon the questions you are asking. For example, the Joseph Chamberlain speech, included under the heading 'Town and country', would also be relevant to questions about Liberal politics, new ideas of democracy and social policy, and so on. Here let me confine myself to a very simple recapitulation.

1 Basic features of the economy

For the fundamental facts you would have to refer to Best and Bédarida. But an important document giving a general sense of optimistic reactions to economic circumstances is the extract from the Course Reader I.7 'Report of Leonard Horner to Lord Palmerston, Home Secretary, 1852'.

2 Social conditions

As we have already noted, Horner's comments on child labour give a rather striking insight into social conditions. To bring yourself into immediate contact with the poverty and misery of Victorian Britain, consult the extracts from the Course Reader I.6 'Henry Mayhew' and I.10 'Notes by the Chief Constable of Staffordshire of a meeting of colliers held at Horsley Heath, Staffordshire, 30 August 1858'.

3   Town and country

The extracts from the Course Reader VI.2 'Reverend Francis Kilvert's diary, 6 May 1870' and VI.5 'Speech of Joseph Chamberlain as Mayor of Birmingham on 13 January 1874' offer valuable insights into aspects of this important heading.

4   Industrialization and social structure

To get a good impression of the development of industrialization, mechanization and the application of technology, read (when you have time) the extract from the Course Reader I.12 'Second report of the Children's Employment Commission, 1864'. For the development of social classes read extract I.13 'R. Dudley Baxter, from *National Income*, 1868' and I.19 'T. H. S. Escott, from *England: Her People, Polity and Pursuits*, 1885'.

5   Culture and belief

You may remember my discussion in section 5 of Unit 1 of the widespread notion of the Victorians as being priggish, prudish, hard working, and so on. From Best, you will have derived a clear view of the importance to them of religion. Extract II.4 'Letter from Charles Darwin to Asa Gray, 22 May 1860' in the Course Reader brings out well the way in which Darwin, despite the scientific evidence, remained extremely reluctant to abandon religion. The two Reform Acts of 1867 and 1884 (extracts V.5 and V.9 in the Course Reader) give direct insights into political values: the cause of representative government was much advanced, yet many restrictions on democracy remained.

6   The major changes in Victorian society from the 1870s onwards

This is one for you to reflect on throughout the rest of the course, particularly as you study literature, art, philosophy and music. However sharp the changes in these areas, can we treat Victorian society as a unity as far as artistic and literary activities are concerned?

It is always good to end on a question mark. Enjoy the remainder of the course, but remember what you have learned about the basic methods of historical study. From time to time, and increasingly in the second part of the course, you will be bringing together what you learn in later units with what you have learned in these three opening units.

8   CONCLUSION

If you have mastered the material discussed during the last three weeks, you should now be much better able:

1   to read history (that is to say, although you are aware that there are bound to be differences of opinion and controversies among historians, you now have a basic idea of how to judge whether one historian is more worth paying attention to than another);

2   to write history (that is to say, given sufficient basic information, you should be able to *plan* and write a short history essay. Your essays will differ from those of other students doing A102 and, of course, different interpretations can be

perfectly acceptable, but you now appreciate that there are also basic principles upon which your tutor can decide whether one essay is better – more historical, more true to how things actually did happen – than another).

8.1   GUIDE TO FURTHER READING

Strangely, there is an almost total dearth of books explaining the basic methods of historical study. However, in 1984 there appeared John Tosh's useful *The Pursuit of History: aims, methods and new directions in the study of history* (Longman) (which takes a particularly sympathetic view of Marxist history). Tosh notes that the only work 'of comparable range' is 'Arthur Marwick's *The Nature of History*, first published in 1970' (in fact there is now a totally revised and rewritten edition, Macmillan 1989, containing much new and up-to-date material) — and that 'the best brief account is the Open University's course booklet, *Introduction to History* (1979), prepared by Arthur Marwick [for A101]'. Tosh describes E. H. Carr's *What is History?* (Penguin, 1964) as 'still unsurpassed as a stimulating and provocative statement by a radically-inclined scholar'. Personally, for reasons given at length in the *Times Higher Education Supplement*, 16 November 1984, I find this an unsatisfactory book. The controversy which followed can be found in the *THES* letter columns for 30 November 1984, 18 January and 1 March 1985. The traditional view of history as seen by a distinguished professional historian can be found in G. R. Elton's *The Practice of History* (Fontana, 1969). *The Historian's Craft* by Marc Bloch (Manchester University Press, 1953) is brilliant, but takes for granted more knowledge than most beginning students possess. For those interested in the more obviously philosophical aspects two excellent books on the nature of historical explanation are: Patrick Gardiner *The Nature of Historical Explanation* (Oxford University Press, 1952) and R. F. Atkinson *Knowledge and Explanation in History* (Macmillan, 1978). There is a full bibliography in my own book, and a briefer one in Tosh's. If you still have doubts about the value of history, then read Marc Ferro's *The Use and Abuse of History* (Routledge, 1984).

REFERENCES

Aldcroft, D. H. (ed.) (1968) *The Development of British Industry and Foreign Competition 1875–1941*, Allen and Unwin.

Bédarida, F. (1979) *A Social History of England 1851–1975*, Methuen. Chapter 4 'The Crisis of Victorian Values' is reprinted in the Supplementary Material booklet.

Best, G. (1979) *Mid-Victorian Britain 1851–75*, Fontana.

Golby, J. (ed.) (1986) *Culture and Society in Britain 1850–1890: a source book of contemporary writings*, Oxford University Press (referred to in the text as the Course Reader).

Hobsbawm, E. J. (1968) *Industry and Empire*, Penguin.

Landes, D. (1969) *The Unbound Prometheus*, Cambridge University Press.

McCloskey, D. N. (1970) 'Did Victorian Britain fail?', *Economic History Review*.

Richardson, H. W. (1968) 'Chemicals' in Aldcroft, D. H. (ed.) (1968).

Sigsworth, E. (1969) 'Some problems in business history', *Sixteenth Business History Conference*.

Thompson, F. M. L. (1963) *English Landed Society in the Nineteenth Century*, Routledge and Kegan Paul. Chapter 10 'The Decline of the Landed Interest, 1830–80' is reprinted in the Supplementary Material booklet.

Wilson, C. (1965) 'Economy and sociology in late Victorian Britain', *Economic History Review*.

ACKNOWLEDGEMENTS

Grateful thanks are given to the following for use of Figures 2–5 (pages 56 and 58): Figures 2 and 3, Museum of London; Figure 4, Windsor Collection; reproduced by gracious permission of Her Majesty the Queen; Figure 5, Photo Godfrey New Photographics Ltd; Corporation of London Records Office.